Common Spaces in Housing Units

ROZANA MONTIEL
ESTUDIO DE
ARQUITECTURA

INFONAVIT

Arquine

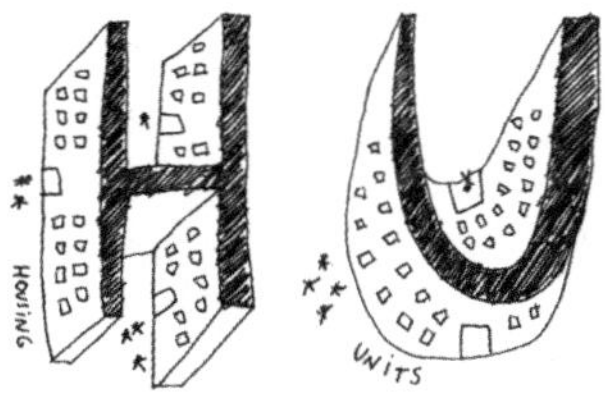

Common Spaces in Housing Units

ROZANA MONTIEL

Plateros Housing Unit, Alvaro Obregón, Mexico City, 2017

Cobre y aluminio Housing Unit, Venustiano Carraza, Mexico City, 2017

HU HU HU HU HU HU HU HU HU HU HU HU HU
HU HU HU HU HU HU HU HU HU HU HU HU HU
HU HU HU HU HU HU HU HU HU HU HU HU HU
HU HU HU HU HU HU HU HU HU HU HU HU HU
HU HU HU HU HU HU HU HU HU HU HU HU HU
HU HU HU HU HU HU
HU HU HU Open space. Space among clouds. HU HU HU
HU HU HU Public space. Space amidst time. HU HU HU
HU HU HU Green space. Space between words. HU HU HU
HU HU HU Vitalspace. Commonspace. Collective HU HU HU
HU HU HU space. Space amid verses. Deserted HU HU HU
HU HU HU space. Woven space. Space among HU HU HU
HU HU HU buildings. Everyday space. Free HU HU HU
HU HU HU space. Uncovered space. Available HU HU HU
HU HU HU space. Sonorous Space. Dream HU HU HU
HU HU HU space. Imaginary space. Inner space. HU HU HU
HU HU HU Outdoor space. Cosmic space. Space HU HU HU
HU HU HU among objects. Place space. Space`s HU HU HU
HU HU HU space. Blank space. Empty space. HU HU HU
HU HU HU HU HU HU HU HU HU HU HU HU HU
HU HU HU HU HU HU HU HU HU HU HU HU HU
HU HU HU HU HU HU HU HU HU HU HU HU HU
HU HU HU HU HU HU HU HU HU HU HU HU HU
HU HU HU HU HU HU HU HU HU HU HU HU HU

The success of a public space project does not only entirely depend on architecture, although good design is key in its performance. These projects are carried out through adequate public policy initiatives and strong institutions with management capacity and inclusive execution processes. Optimal results require plural and multidisciplinary teams to serve and improve conditions for end users.

It is therefore important to acknowledge the public policy behind these projects. In this case, which is the result of a pledge made by Mexico's President, Enrique Peña Nieto, who commited to develop a maintenance program at the main housing projects in Mexico City, in his Commitment No. 200.

"Mejorando la Unidad" (Retrofitting Housing Projects) was a program developed as part of this commitment with the aim of upgrading the living conditions in housing projects at the same time as making interventions in their common or public spaces. This program was designed by the Institute of the National Housing Fund for Workers (Infonavit) and implemented through its current Research Center for Sustainable Development (CIDS), in conjunction with the Ministry of Agrarian, Territorial and Urban Development (SEDATU), the Federal Mortgage Society (SHF), the National Housing Commission (CONAVI), the Government of Mexico City (CDMX) and local administrations of each City borough.

Various aspects were vital for the proper implementation of the project, making it possible to identify people's needs as a community and the physical state of the public spaces chosen for interventions. This phase involved two essential processes before the intervention of the architect. Firstly, a social cohesion study assessed the extent of urban poverty due to the lack of communication and trust among residents. Public resources were therefore earmarked to tackle this problem by improving physical spaces and social relationships. To gauge the level of social cohesion inside the housing project, a "vulnerability survey" was designed to gather information about general aspects of each project: social polarization, social networks, collective action, decision-making within the project, and the profile of the families living there. The second process was a physical analysis carried out by the Architecture School at the National Autonomous University of Mexico (UNAM), who conducted a research into the physical condition of more than 400 housing projects in Mexico City. This analysis considered various factors, including the housing projects' location within a specific urban context, area and population; the level of social development among local inhabitants; the area's socio-economic and demographic structure; and characteristics of common space: its component elements, use and state of maintenance.

This information was delivered to the architect commissioned to execute the project, thus providing an essential understanding of the housing project to be worked with, as well as the local context detonating architects' professional approach before they heard the specific needs of locals and residents directly for themselves. After taking on board this information and local requests, an understanding was reached with the community itself and the local authorities to ensure that the project was properly implemented, in compliance with the local regulations and zoning laws.

As a result, "Mejorando la Unidad" not only achieved its goal of establishing a program of improvements for Mexico City's main housing projects, but it also went beyond geographical boundaries of Mexico's capital. Through Infonavit, interventions were carried out on more than 200 public spaces, following the same scheme and involving hundreds of professionals given this opportunity to make greater contribution to society through their professional work.

The interventions by the architect Rozana Montiel, whose successful projects are shown here, are not only celebrated by those of us who created the initiatives to make this project happen, but by the thousands of residents and continual national and international awards. They provide an example of how things can be done well in Mexico, how properly implemented public policies improve citizens' quality of life, and how applied research can improve public policy initiatives.

Carlos Zedillo Velasco
Head of the Research Center of Sustainable Development

* HU:

HU (Housing Units) refers to Housing States or Housing Developments.

COMMON SPACES IN HOUSING UNITS

Create a sense of common unity. Transform space into place. Inhabit time. Search for content in context. Transform the vertical to horizontal. Changes barriers to boundaries. Reconstruct habitability. Restore unity to the community.

Housing Units (HU*) compiles the research requested by Infonavit to Rozana Montiel Estudio de Arquitectura (REA) in more than twenty Housing Units and the rehabilitation of public spaces of three of them, in different geographies and contexts: Common-Unity in Mexico City, Court in Veracruz and Fresnillo Playground in Zacatecas.

The structure of the book is constructed through alphabetically ordered words, graphic aphorisms contained in three hundred and fifty post-its, photos and spatial poetry. The compilation forms a glossary. The book seeks to re-signify different ways of interacting in the HU's.

The three projects interweave images and aphorisms contained in the post-its, as well as the twenty-six alphabet letters that identify its contexts. The spatial poetry suggests a typographic construction of ideas.

The book may be read in fragments, starting on any page or consulted in a ludic way: its different readings multiply the narrative.

The series of graphic aphorisms contained in the post-its are at the same time process and results: they give a non-linear understanding of the projects, though a thematic one; it is a way of looking at reality to transform it.

HU is a book-object, a succession of clues, a game of words, a glossary of motifs, a photographic archive, a method to theorize about space, a manual on how to interact in common spaces, a guide on how to read the texts and sub-texts of public space.

Rozana Montiel

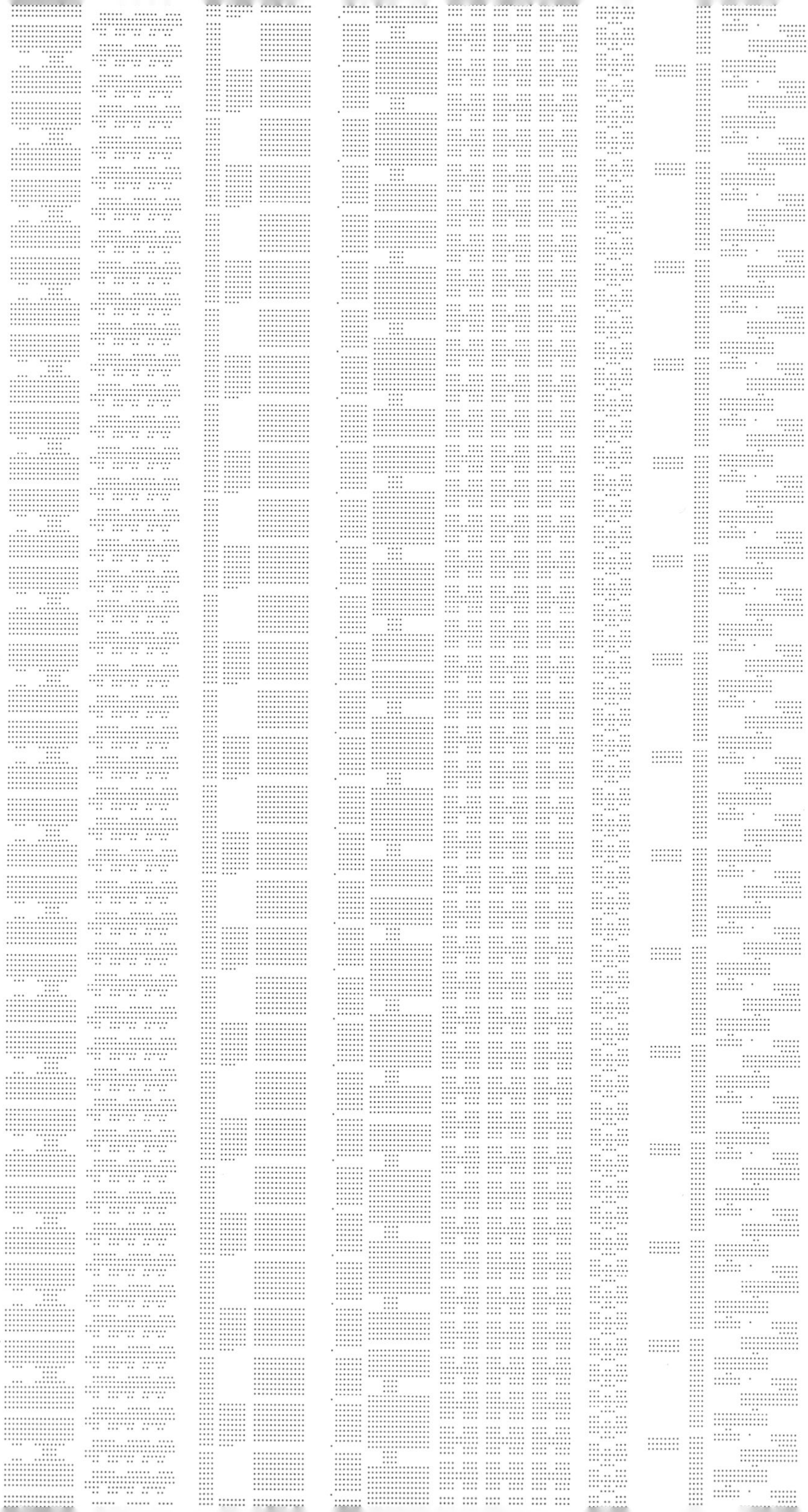

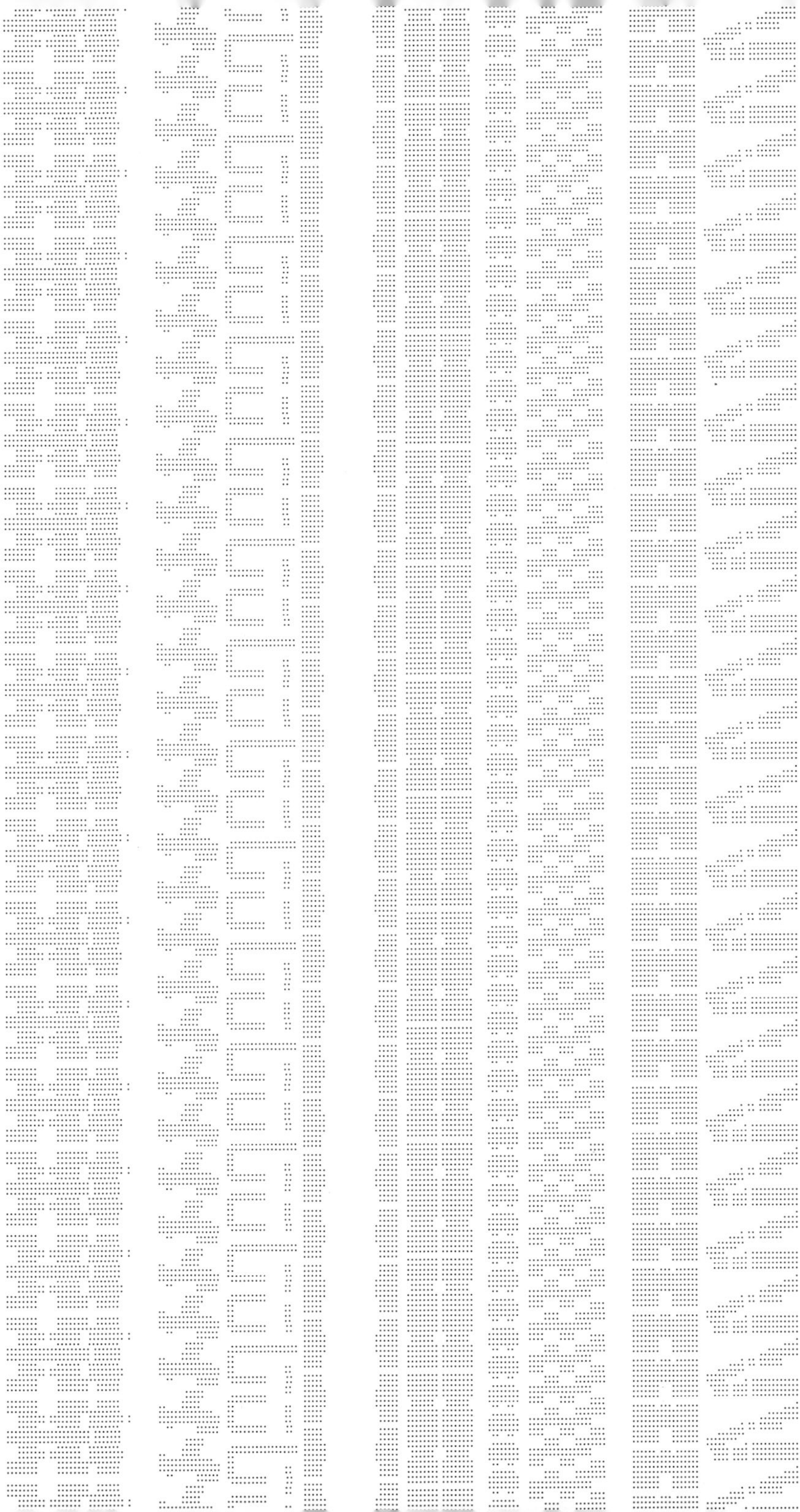

Mexico City's Housing Units Footprints

ACTION

A

An active public space reactivates the deoxyribonucleic acid (DNA) in the city.

Public events such as site-actions change the local atmosphere. Their resonance produces in space an overall change of perception.

Every action casts an impression amongst the community to transform and redefine public space.

Through games and experimentation, public actions allow that the community of the HU to explore strategies of development with few elements.

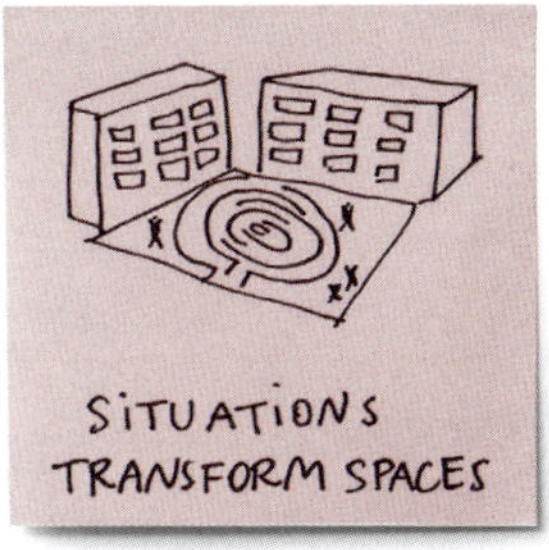

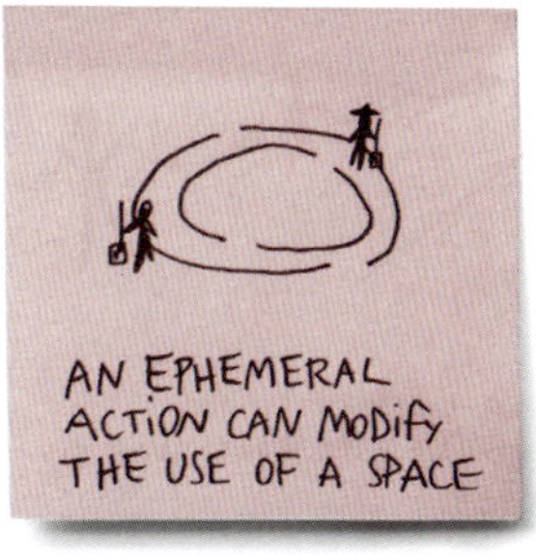

Site-actions are low-cost interventions that involve people within their space in ephemeral, ludic and innovative ways. Their objective is to express people´s needs and aspirations.

SITE-ACTIONS ARE
LOW BUDGET PROJECTS

A CHALK LINE CAN
SUGGEST A PATHWAY

A LINE OF LIGHTS
GENERATE A PATHWAY TOO

Through low-cost, medium-scale, meaningful interventions, in different layers, it is possible to achieve large-scale renewal developments to reshape the HU complexes as economic drivers.

We believe architectural thinking meets resilience in the face of rubble: when the building effort shifts its meaning from laying bricks to relieving, releasing, reusing, recycling, recovering, re-signifying, relating, rectifying, replying, rethinking, reflecting, recruiting, readapting, replacing, re-locating, receding, re-developing, reabsorbing, re-working, remembering, recreating, rediscovering, reforming, renegotiating, reinterpreting, rehabilitating we create space for action.

Design process activates space through interaction.

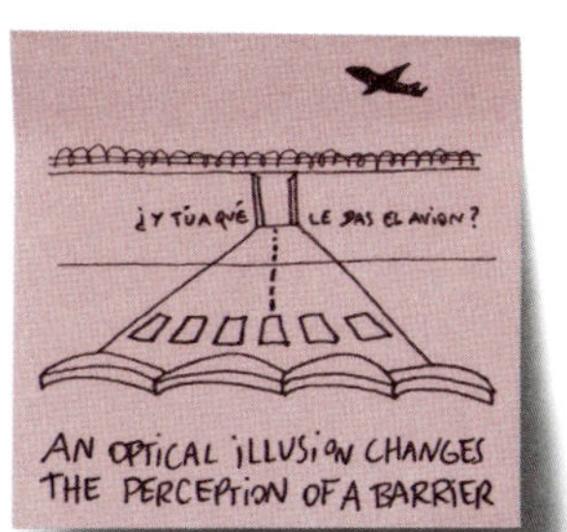

Labyrinth: urban action by REA,Gustavo A. Madero, Mexico City

The street-peddler is an urban event that engages the surrounding community and enables us to understand people's itineraries, cycles, and rhythms.

The ambulant, embedded in the informal economy, lives on the margins of institutional regulation. Hawkers hinge on freedom, allowing democratic relationships necessary to the social fabric; his capacity to improvise a sui-generis space wherever he goes, makes his daily activity, in and of itself, a provoking re-examination of traditional spatial assumptions concerning exchange and habitation for mobility.

AMBULANT

A

…et-peddlers not only of… unique reading of the …n space, but they also …ome a dynamic way …nderstand community …ds with their space. …r trade practices serve …n original approach to …itectonic design that …ts to improvisation, im…manence, and inventive… that directly addresses … needs, resources and …ctions.

CALLE GONZALEZ ECHEVER
316 COL. OLIVAR
minisuper
Corona

Fresnillo Playground : Housing Unit public space project by REA, Fresnillo, Zacatecas, 2017

What is remembered
What is wished.

What is lent.

What is liked.
What is given.

What matters.
What works.

What it means.

What I make mine.

When space becomes a place, the community identifies with it, takes advantage of it, maintains it, cleans it and takes care of it.

When the design of a public space expresses the functional and integral needs of a community, its inhabitants develop a sense of ownership and pride.

APPROPRIATION

A

HU inhabitants usually seize up every square inch of the public space: they invade it and, therefore, it deteriorates.

Social conflicts are the result of an appropriation of public space.

Whenever a community is involved in a project, once finished, it becomes theirs, and they tend to keep it in good condition thus lasting in time.

Our projects facilitated a different kind of ownership and appropriation: one that habituates inhabitants to work for the common good.

Clotheslines, Legaria Housing Unit, Miguel Hidalgo, Mexico City, 2017

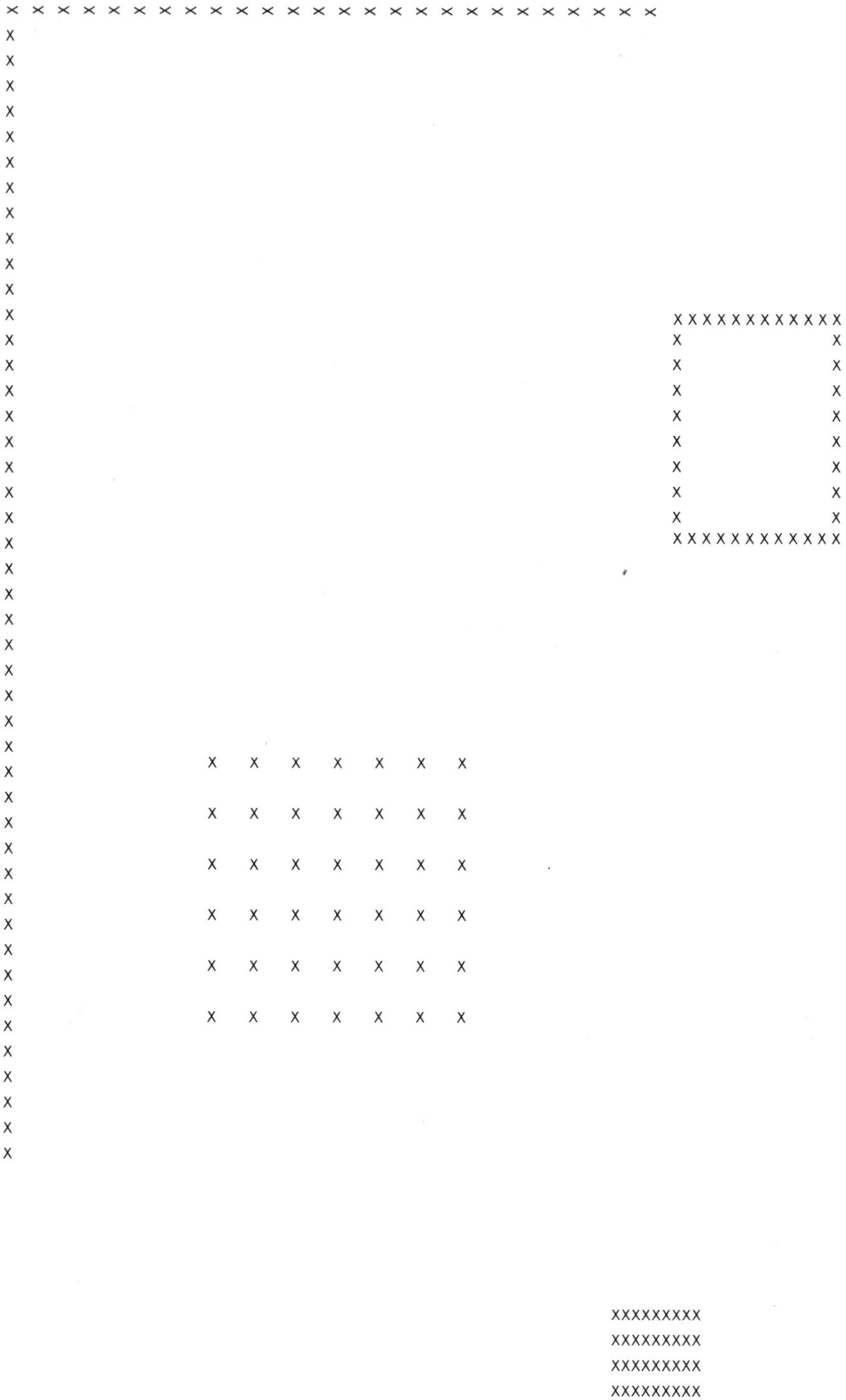

BARRIERS

B

Barriers tend to block movement, learning, and commerce: they are not only physical but psychological and geographical.

In many of our projects, we found sectioned HU, where the original zoning and entrances had been altered by fences and barriers built by their inhabitants over time.

There is an ongoing discussion about building barriers and walls to define physical borders and limits. These concerns are directly related to any architect's occupation.

In Mexico, due to safety issues, both private property and public space are protected by railings, walls, and fences. This phenomenon is unjustified when protection itself becomes a barrier.

By eliminating vertical structures such as walls, gates, and barriers, the community binds together. The use of horizontal surfaces supports the idea of sheltering instead of dividing.

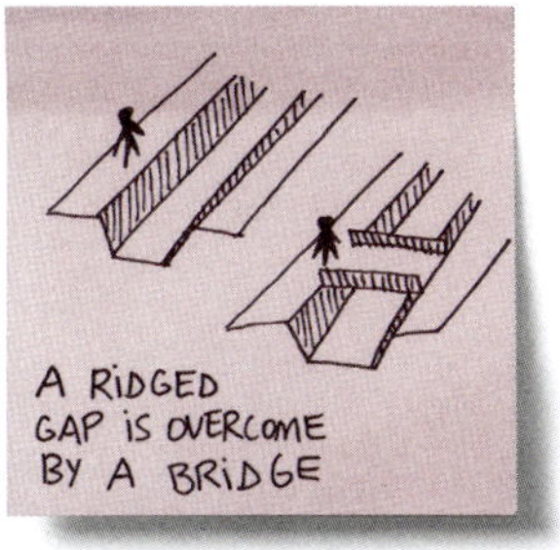

Poor social integration skills are the result of the lack of adequate public spaces. HU blocks are notorious for having barriers that owners define as limits.

B

U

O

N D

R

A

E

I

S

BOUNDARIES

B

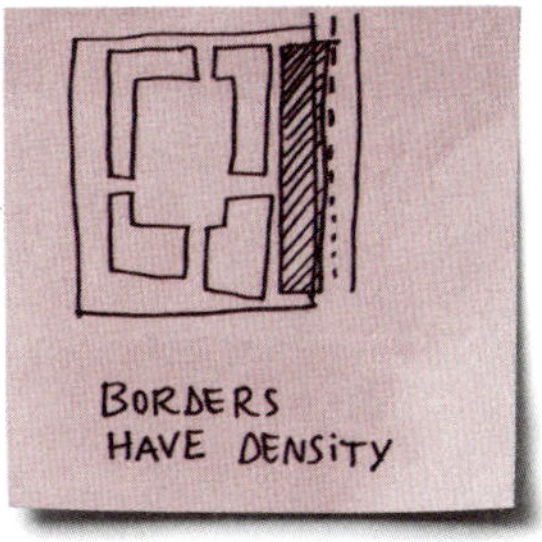

Boundaries are inhabitable borders or horizons.
Change barriers to boundaries: build trust. While barriers lock everyone further into conflict, limits require people to communicate aspirations as well as delicate issues.

Designing for boundaries assists in the clear expression of everyone's values, ultimately empowering community as a whole.

Boundaries between open spaces and enclosures conflate in many fluctuations.
We interact through boundaries; we integrate opportunity, we involve everyone's presence.

Dissolving a barrier to a boundary produces a change in the focus of perception: the immediate appropriation of the place, the social cohesion, the integration of limits, and the spatial freedom of the horizontal in architecture.

Before the Fresnillo Playground intervention

esnillo Playground: Housing Unit public space project by REA, Fresnillo, Zacatecas, 2017

CITY

A city is a place where sites, subjects, actions, and objects interact. As a container of industrial structures, as an archive of tales and stories that interweave with people`s itineraries, the city becomes a warehouse for site-actions.

Mexico City is home to a multiplicity of cities. Its housing complexes are massive: 25% of the population lives in housing units. Such compounds are cities themselves.

If we think of the cityscape not as a form but as a system, the impact of renovated public space in HU amounts to a long-term ripple-effect that transforms the cultural landscape of the city.

To revitalize the "underdreamed" space, we collaborate and work out ideas with real people in different places and cities.

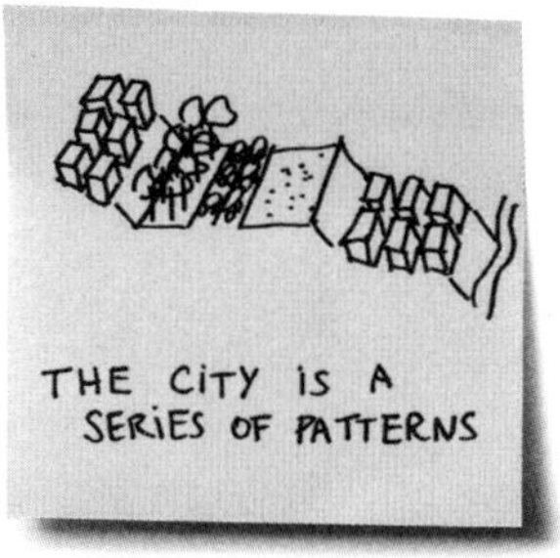

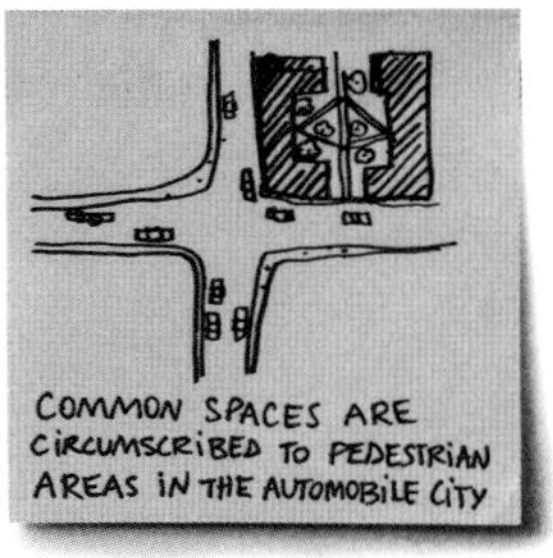

"People build a house to live in it, people found a city to leave their house and meet others who have also left theirs."

Ortega y Gasset

Ixtapaluca Housing Units and the surrounding city, Mexico City

Changing loud, aggressive colors commonly used on HU to a more earthen palette helps people feel more welcome on the urban scale.

A simple change of color makes people feel as if they have moved to a different place: color gives them a sense of a fresh start.

COLOR

Dramatic changes in the city space are achieved through the mere use of color.

The use of color in architecture creates atmospheres, modifying the perception of space and emotions toward it.

Drawing lines of color on the ground inspires a whole range of activities: games, limits, figures, and designs.

New comers bring new commerce.

Trade within HU generates a formal and informal economy, an exchange of skills and goods.

People use every single corner of available space, even a window or a door to sell meals, drinks, used furniture and other goods.

Residents sell all sorts of services: meal services, beauty salons, mechanic workshop and repairs, medical facilities. All kinds of craftsmanship are offered: masons, carpenters, hair stylists, teachers.

Urban objects and temporary structures such as posts, tarps and wooden crates, are used to facilitate trade modifying the aspect and urban operation of the sites.

COMMERCE

C

COMMERCE IS ENGAGED WHEREVER POSSIBLE

STAIRCASE NOOKS TURN INTO HANG-OUT AND COMMERCIAL AREAS

SOME COVER UP THEIR APARTMENT WINDOWS TO FURNISH A SHOP

GROUND FLOOR FACADES BECOME MERCHANDISE DISPLAY CASES

BUILDING ENTRANCES ARE LINED WITH SHOPS

Entrance to Heroes de Granaditas Housing Unit, Cuauhtémoc, Mexico City, 2015

CONVERSE
CONVERSE
CONVERSE
CONVERSE
CONVERSE
NIKE

COMMON-UNITY

COMMUNITY

COMMUNALITIES

COLLECTIVES

COMMUNITY

C

Community engagement is a crucial element to activate and sustain a public space.

By efficiently activating the public space in HU, a grassroots culture can, therefore, emerge and shape the community.

Community building engages and shapes civic action in public spaces as an anchor for equity, diversity, and resilience.

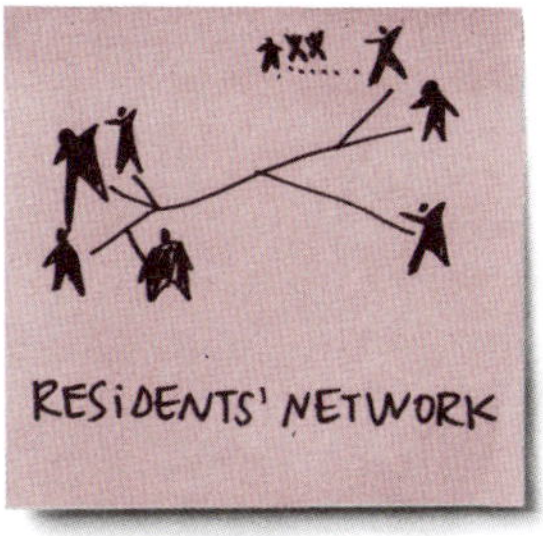

Rehabilitating public space restores the community's use of it, transforming public space into common place.

In a restored public space violence decreases, enabling a more harmonious cohabitation.

Reshaping public space together with a community helps reknit the social fabric.

Fresnillo Playground: Housing Unit public space project by REA, Fresnillo, Zacatecas, 2017

An expanded program engages different age groups and audiences, proving more effective in the restoration of the social fabric that activates a community.

Cross-programming allows a more efficient trade, information and knowledge exchange.

CROSS-PROGRAMMING

C

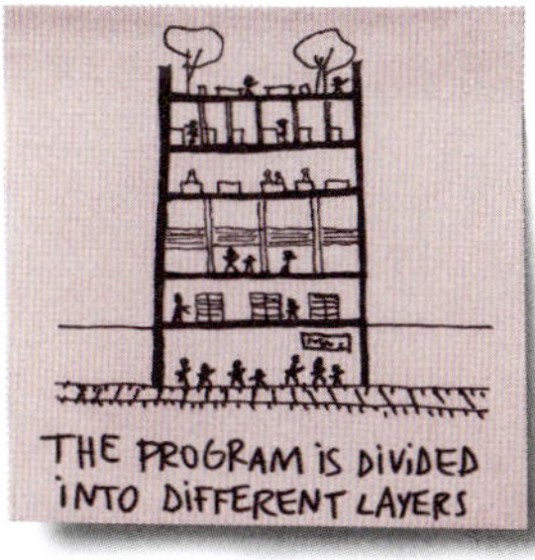

Cross-programming densifies urban economic activity, reduces commuting distances, allows people to spend more time with their family, commuting health and education. It capitalizes sustainable pedestrian environments and transit mobility avoiding urban sprawl.

Cross-programming is about expanding the program for mixed functions and temporal uses in compact spaces.

Court: Housing Unit public space project by REA,Lagos de Puente Moreno, Veracruz, 2016

l a t t i c e
l a t t i c e
l a t t i c e
l a t t i c e
l a t t i c e
l a t t i c e
l a t t i c e
l a t t i c e
l a t t i c e
l a t t i c e
l a t t i c e
l a t t i c e

t: Housing Unit public space project by REA,Lagos de Puente Moreno, Veracruz, 2016

EVERY INHABITANT
HAS SKILLS

TO FUNCTION PROPERLY,
SPACE REQUIRES
EVERYONE'S COLLABORATION

PETS ARE ALSO HU
INHABITANTS

A RAMP IS AN
INCLUSIVE ELEMENT

COMMON SPACES ARE
OPPORTUNITIES TO
ENCOUNTER DIVERSITY

DIVERSITY

D

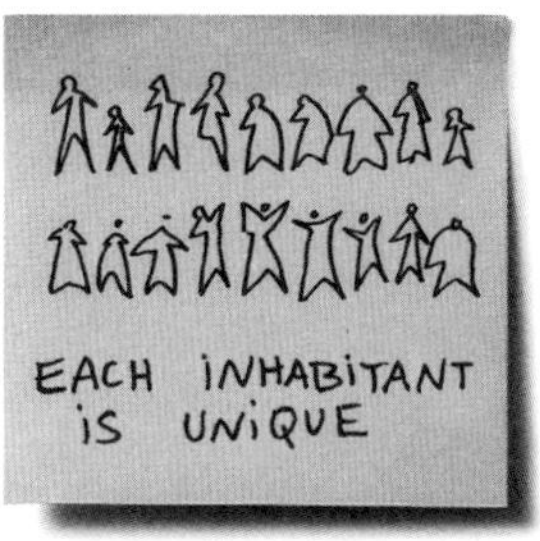

Diversity is inclusive in its abundance.

Diversity allows residents of an HU to dispose of, modify and even personalize private space to make it stand out from others inside the compound.

A tactic is a prototype temporary solution that gradually builds spaces for diversity, benefiting from informality to engage the community.

Unclaimed urban spaces may be transformed into inclusive places, rich in functional diversity.

The diversity of elements (color, vegetation, games, shops) in each sector of the HU, maintains the neighborhood character.

The diversity of daily activities of the inhabitant in the public space improves their quality of life and promotes interaction.

Ecotones that result from recycling are great for place-making programs.

The urban ecotone, as a transition zone with a border effect, offers greater possibilities for the use of productive intersections. These intersections produce a third space, with great potential for the creation of new scenarios.

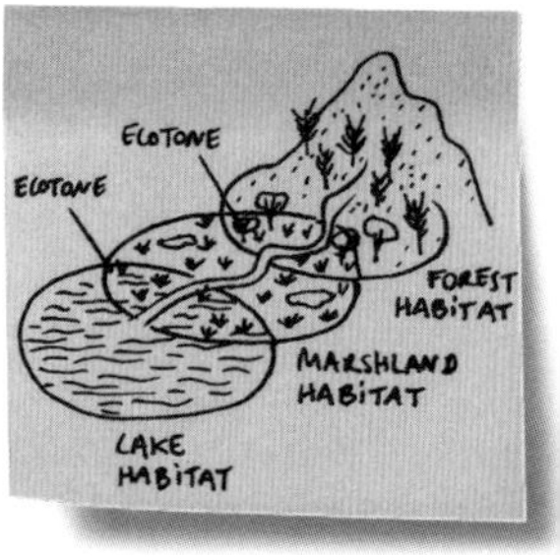

ECOTONE

E

Biologically speaking, the ecotone is a transitional territory, which modulates the tension arising between two distinct environments.

In urban and architectural design, an ecotone is a place that harmoniously merges the public and private spheres, tempering the transition from open space to enclosed areas, allowing respectful co-existence of built-up and the natural regions.

Recycling and re-signifying the infrastructure of a site is the best way to create an ecotone.

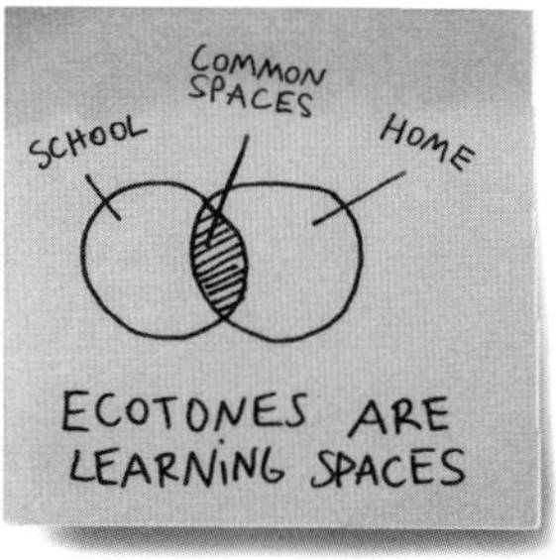

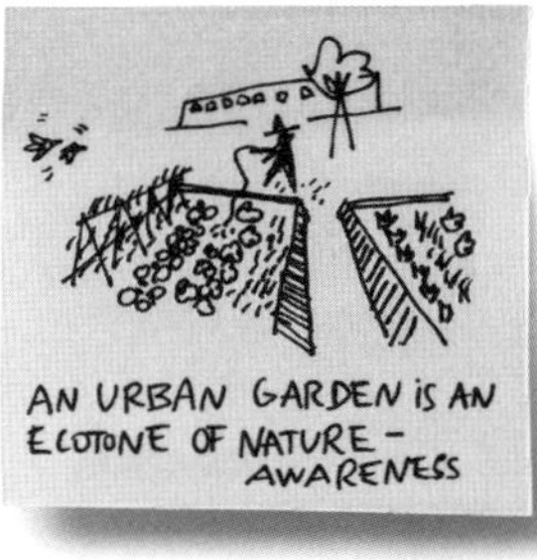

Court: Housing Unit public space project by REA, Lagos de Puente Moreno, Veracruz, 2016

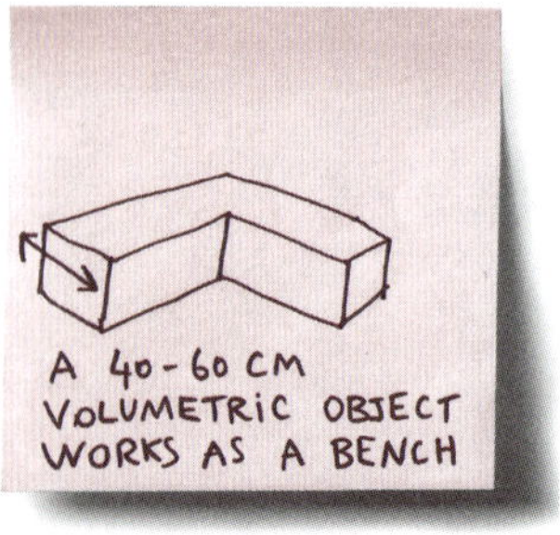

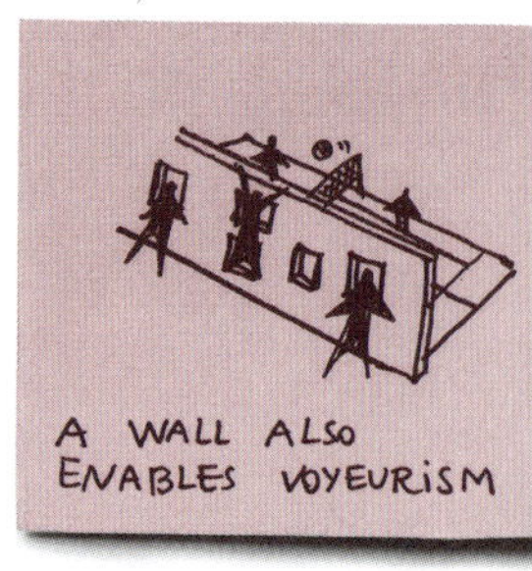

Movement in architecture allows flexible configurations.

FLEXIBILITY

Program expansion aims to enrich enrich interaction between people.

Spaces designed by us are multifunctional, housing many activities whatever their size; all of them are appealing areas for different age-groups to be used at different times during the day.

For example: in between the columns of a roof, we inserted a multi-functional program comprising swings, hammocks, library, computer room, restrooms, forum and a playground.

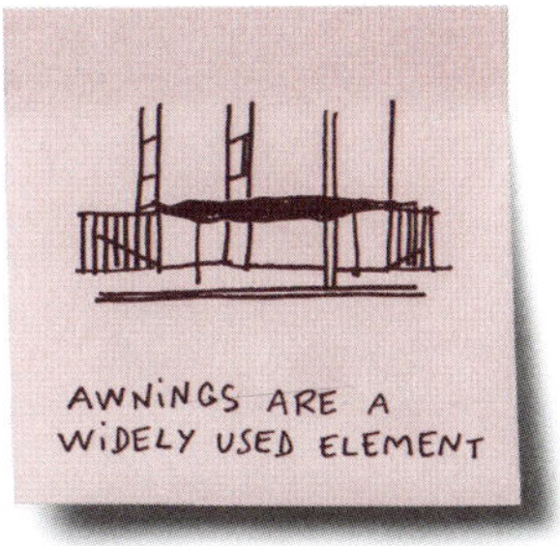

t : Housing Unit public space project by REA,Lagos de Puente Moreno, Veracruz, 2016

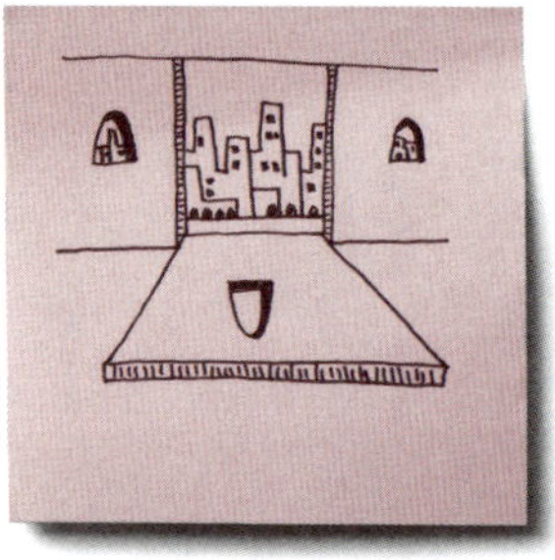

We have set free various public spaces fragmented by different types of barriers. The goal has been to eliminate the obstacles that block these spaces, spatially demarcating them.

The strategy has consisted of exchanging the vertical (railing, walls, enclosure) that separates and divides, with the horizontal (roof, cover, floor patterns, common ground) that unites, reunites, brings closer, and encourages social interaction. It is a way of reclaiming a privatized place to generate a common good.

The wall becomes a floor: the backdrop reconnects to the foreground. By deconstructing the wall, the public realm integrates with the private sphere. Barriers, transformed into a horizontal structure, support horizons. A fence is also an opening, a passageway, a door, a window. Our project reveals the integration of different territories on both sides of a barrier. We free space through a shift of perception: the wall is re-enacted as a connective infrastructure.

FREESPACE

F

A free-space opening that connects the inside of the building with the outside. Creates continuity. Frees the sky-light to become an exit, a doorway, a passage-way, a threshold, a bridge, a lookout, an outlook.

To free the potential of space for it to become "a place" follows the belief that architecture is also a social construction.

Free-space translates into Spanish as a word game: it means, "Set space free/ libera espacio," and "leeway for action/espacio libre."

Free-space is both the imperative to act and space for action, the latent potential to develop a place.

To free-space, one first must set free space by removing not physical barriers but also geographic ones.

The horizontal is more than just a roof: it is a free, multi-functional platform that makes it possible for sports, recreational and cultural activities to take place in common areas (games, reading, studying, theater presentations, film projections, conferences, dance classes, and relaxation).

Court: Housing Unit public space project by REA, Lagos de Puente Moreno, Veracruz, 2016

Playground areas for kids and teens are essential to bond a community.

Games allow instants of reality and fiction, time and scale changes.

Leisure time and recreational spaces for everyone should be an equity principle.

The game encourages diversion (other versions of reality) that stimulate creativity, learning processes and community building. stimulate creativity, learning processes and community building.

The game allows the appropriation of the physical or virtual space; thus transformed into a private act or a collective expression.

Common-Unity: Housing Unit public space project by REA, Azcapotzalco, Mexico City, 2015-2016

XXXXXXXXXXXXXXXXXXXXXXXXXXXX
XXXXXXXXXXXXXXXXXXXXXXXXXXXX
XXXXXXXXXXXXXXXXXXXXXXXXXXXX
XXXXXXXXXXXXXXXXXXXXXXXXXXXX
XXXXXXXXXXXXXXXXXXXXXXXXXXXX
XXXXXXXXXXXXXXXXXXXXXXXXXXXX
XXXXXXXXXXXXXXXXXXXXXXXXXXXX
XXXXXXXXXXXXXXXXXXXXXXXXXXXX
XXXXXXXXXXXXXXXXXXXXXXXXXXXX
XXXXXXXXXXXXXXXXXXXXXXXXXXXX
XXXXXXXXXXXXXXXXXXXXXXXXXXXX
XXXXXXXXXXXXXXXXXXXXXXXXXXXX

XXXXXXXXXXXXXXXXXXXXXXXXXXXX
XXXXXXXXXXXXXXXXXXXXXXXXXXXX
XXXXXXXXXXXXXXXXXXXXXXXXXXXX
XXXXXXXXXXXXXXXXXXXXXXXXXXXX
XXXXXXXXXXXXXXXXXXXXXXXXXXXX
XXXXXXXXXXXXXXXXXXXXXXXXXXXX
XXXXXXXXXXXXXXXXXXXXXXXXXXXX
XXXXXXXXXXXXXXXXXXXXXXXXXXXX
XXXXXXXXXXXXXXXXXXXXXXXXXXXX
XXXXXXXXXXXXXXXXXXXXXXXXXXXX
XXXXXXXXXXXXXXXXXXXXXXXXXXXX
XXXXXXXXXXXXXXXXXXXXXXXXXXXX

XXXXXXXXXXXXXXXXXXXXXXXXXXXX
XXXXXXXXXXXXXXXXXXXXXXXXXXXX
XXXXXXXXXXXXXXXXXXXXXXXXXXXX
XXXXXXXXXXXXXXXXXXXXXXXXXXXX
XXXXXXXXXXXXXXXXXXXXXXXXXXXX
XXXXXXXXXXXXXXXXXXXXXXXXXXXX
XXXXXXXXXXXXXXXXXXXXXXXXXXXX
XXXXXXXXXXXXXXXXXXXXXXXXXXXX
XXXXXXXXXXXXXXXXXXXXXXXXXXXX
XXXXXXXXXXXXXXXXXXXXXXXXXXXX
XXXXXXXXXXXXXXXXXXXXXXXXXXXX
XXXXXXXXXXXXXXXXXXXXXXXXXXXX

XXXXXXXXXXXXXXXXXXXXXXXXXXXX
XXXXXXXXXXXXXXXXXXXXXXXXXXXX
XXXXXXXXXXXXXXXXXXXXXXXXXXXX
XXXXXXXXXXXXXXXXXXXXXXXXXXXX
XXXXXXXXXXXXXXXXXXXXXXXXXXXX
XXXXXXXXXXXXXXXXXXXXXXXXXXXX
XXXXXXXXXXXXXXXXXXXXXXXXXXXX
XXXXXXXXXXXXXXXXXXXXXXXXXXXX
XXXXXXXXXXXXXXXXXXXXXXXXXXXX
XXXXXXXXXXXXXXXXXXXXXXXXXXXX
XXXXXXXXXXXXXXXXXXXXXXXXXXXX
XXXXXXXXXXXXXXXXXXXXXXXXXXXX

XXXXXXXXXXXXXXXXXXXXXXXXXXXX
XXXXXXXXXXXXXXXXXXXXXXXXXXXX
XXXXXXXXXXXXXXXXXXXXXXXXXXXX
XXXXXXXXXXXXXXXXXXXXXXXXXXXX
XXXXXXXXXXXXXXXXXXXXXXXXXXXX
XXXXXXXXXXXXXXXXXXXXXXXXXXXX
XXXXXXXXXXXXXXXXXXXXXXXXXXXX
XXXXXXXXXXXXXXXXXXXXXXXXXXXX
XXXXXXXXXXXXXXXXXXXXXXXXXXXX
XXXXXXXXXXXXXXXXXXXXXXXXXXXX
XXXXXXXXXXXXXXXXXXXXXXXXXXXX
XXXXXXXXXXXXXXXXXXXXXXXXXXXX

XXXXXXXXXXXXXXXXXXXXXXXXXXXX
XXXXXXXXXXXXXXXXXXXXXXXXXXXX
XXXXXXXXXXXXXXXXXXXXXXXXXXXX
XXXXXXXXXXXXXXXXXXXXXXXXXXXX
XXXXXXXXXXXXXXXXXXXXXXXXXXXX
XXXXXXXXXXXXXXXXXXXXXXXXXXXX
XXXXXXXXXXXXXXXXXXXXXXXXXXXX
XXXXXXXXXXXXXXXXXXXXXXXXXXXX
XXXXXXXXXXXXXXXXXXXXXXXXXXXX
XXXXXXXXXXXXXXXXXXXXXXXXXXXX
XXXXXXXXXXXXXXXXXXXXXXXXXXXX
XXXXXXXXXXXXXXXXXXXXXXXXXXXX

XXXXXXXXXXXXXXXXXXXXXXXXXXXX
XXXXXXXXXXXXXXXXXXXXXXXXXXXX
XXXXXXXXXXXXXXXXXXXXXXXXXXXX
XXXXXXXXXXXXXXXXXXXXXXXXXXXX
XXXXXXXXXXXXXXXXXXXXXXXXXXXX
XXXXXXXXXXXXXXXXXXXXXXXXXXXX
XXXXXXXXXXXXXXXXXXXXXXXXXXXX
XXXXXXXXXXXXXXXXXXXXXXXXXXXX
XXXXXXXXXXXXXXXXXXXXXXXXXXXX
XXXXXXXXXXXXXXXXXXXXXXXXXXXX
XXXXXXXXXXXXXXXXXXXXXXXXXXXX
XXXXXXXXXXXXXXXXXXXXXXXXXXXX

XXXXXXXXXXXXXXXXXXXXXXXXXXXX
XXXXXXXXXXXXXXXXXXXXXXXXXXXX
XXXXXXXXXXXXXXXXXXXXXXXXXXXX
XXXXXXXXXXXXXXXXXXXXXXXXXXXX
XXXXXXXXXXXXXXXXXXXXXXXXXXXX
XXXXXXXXXXXXXXXXXXXXXXXXXXXX
XXXXXXXXXXXXXXXXXXXXXXXXXXXX
XXXXXXXXXXXXXXXXXXXXXXXXXXXX
XXXXXXXXXXXXXXXXXXXXXXXXXXXX
XXXXXXXXXXXXXXXXXXXXXXXXXXXX
XXXXXXXXXXXXXXXXXXXXXXXXXXXX
XXXXXXXXXXXXXXXXXXXXXXXXXXXX

XXXXXXXXXXXXXXXXXXXXXXXXXXXX
XXXXXXXXXXXXXXXXXXXXXXXXXXXX
XXXXXXXXXXXXXXXXXXXXXXXXXXXX
XXXXXXXXXXXXXXXXXXXXXXXXXXXX
XXXXXXXXXXXXXXXXXXXXXXXXXXXX
XXXXXXXXXXXXXXXXXXXXXXXXXXXX
XXXXXXXXXXXXXXXXXXXXXXXXXXXX
XXXXXXXXXXXXXXXXXXXXXXXXXXXX
XXXXXXXXXXXXXXXXXXXXXXXXXXXX
XXXXXXXXXXXXXXXXXXXXXXXXXXXX
XXXXXXXXXXXXXXXXXXXXXXXXXXXX
XXXXXXXXXXXXXXXXXXXXXXXXXXXX

XXXXXXXXXXXXXXXXXXXXXXXXXXXX
XXXXXXXXXXXXXXXXXXXXXXXXXXXX
XXXXXXXXXXXXXXXXXXXXXXXXXXXX
XXXXXXXXXXXXXXXXXXXXXXXXXXXX
XXXXXXXXXXXXXXXXXXXXXXXXXXXX
XXXXXXXXXXXXXXXXXXXXXXXXXXXX
XXXXXXXXXXXXXXXXXXXXXXXXXXXX
XXXXXXXXXXXXXXXXXXXXXXXXXXXX
XXXXXXXXXXXXXXXXXXXXXXXXXXXX
XXXXXXXXXXXXXXXXXXXXXXXXXXXX
XXXXXXXXXXXXXXXXXXXXXXXXXXXX
XXXXXXXXXXXXXXXXXXXXXXXXXXXX

XXXXXXXXXXXXXXXXXXXXXXXXXXXX
XXXXXXXXXXXXXXXXXXXXXXXXXXXX
XXXXXXXXXXXXXXXXXXXXXXXXXXXX
XXXXXXXXXXXXXXXXXXXXXXXXXXXX
XXXXXXXXXXXXXXXXXXXXXXXXXXXX
XXXXXXXXXXXXXXXXXXXXXXXXXXXX
XXXXXXXXXXXXXXXXXXXXXXXXXXXX
XXXXXXXXXXXXXXXXXXXXXXXXXXXX
XXXXXXXXXXXXXXXXXXXXXXXXXXXX
XXXXXXXXXXXXXXXXXXXXXXXXXXXX
XXXXXXXXXXXXXXXXXXXXXXXXXXXX
XXXXXXXXXXXXXXXXXXXXXXXXXXXX

XXXXXXXXXXXXXXXXXXXXXXXXXXXX
XXXXXXXXXXXXXXXXXXXXXXXXXXXX
XXXXXXXXXXXXXXXXXXXXXXXXXXXX
XXXXXXXXXXXXXXXXXXXXXXXXXXXX
XXXXXXXXXXXXXXXXXXXXXXXXXXXX
XXXXXXXXXXXXXXXXXXXXXXXXXXXX
XXXXXXXXXXXXXXXXXXXXXXXXXXXX
XXXXXXXXXXXXXXXXXXXXXXXXXXXX
XXXXXXXXXXXXXXXXXXXXXXXXXXXX
XXXXXXXXXXXXXXXXXXXXXXXXXXXX
XXXXXXXXXXXXXXXXXXXXXXXXXXXX
XXXXXXXXXXXXXXXXXXXXXXXXXXXX

XXXXXXXXXXXXXXXXXXXXXXXXXXX
XXXXXXXXXXXXXXXXXXXXXXXXXXX
XXXXXXXXXXXXXXXXXXXXXXXXXXX
XXXXXXXXXXXXXXXXXXXXXXXXXXX
XXXXXXXXXXXXXXXXXXXXXXXXXXX
XXXXXXXXXXXXXXXXXXXXXXXXXXX
XXXXXXXXXXXXXXXXXXXXXXXXXXX
XXXXXXXXXXXXXXXXXXXXXXXXXXX
XXXXXXXXXXXXXXXXXXXXXXXXXXX
XXXXXXXXXXXXXXXXXXXXXXXXXXX
XXXXXXXXXXXXXXXXXXXXXXXXXXX
XXXXXXXXXXXXXXXXXXXXXXXXXXX

XXXXXXXXXXXXXXXXXXXXXXXXXXX
XXXXXXXXXXXXXXXXXXXXXXXXXXX
XXXXXXXXXXXXXXXXXXXXXXXXXXX
XXXXXXXXXXXXXXXXXXXXXXXXXXX
XXXXXXXXXXXXXXXXXXXXXXXXXXX
XXXXXXXXXXXXXXXXXXXXXXXXXXX
XXXXXXXXXXXXXXXXXXXXXXXXXXX
XXXXXXXXXXXXXXXXXXXXXXXXXXX
XXXXXXXXXXXXXXXXXXXXXXXXXXX
XXXXXXXXXXXXXXXXXXXXXXXXXXX
XXXXXXXXXXXXXXXXXXXXXXXXXXX
XXXXXXXXXXXXXXXXXXXXXXXXXXX

XXXXXXXXXXXXXXXXXXXXXXXXXXX
XXXXXXXXXXXXXXXXXXXXXXXXXXX
XXXXXXXXXXXXXXXXXXXXXXXXXXX
XXXXXXXXXXXXXXXXXXXXXXXXXXX
XXXXXXXXXXXXXXXXXXXXXXXXXXX
XXXXXXXXXXXXXXXXXXXXXXXXXXX
XXXXXXXXXXXXXXXXXXXXXXXXXXX
XXXXXXXXXXXXXXXXXXXXXXXXXXX
XXXXXXXXXXXXXXXXXXXXXXXXXXX
XXXXXXXXXXXXXXXXXXXXXXXXXXX
XXXXXXXXXXXXXXXXXXXXXXXXXXX
XXXXXXXXXXXXXXXXXXXXXXXXXXX

Cars in gated parking, Housing Unit, 2016

GRASS AREAS
GET FENCED

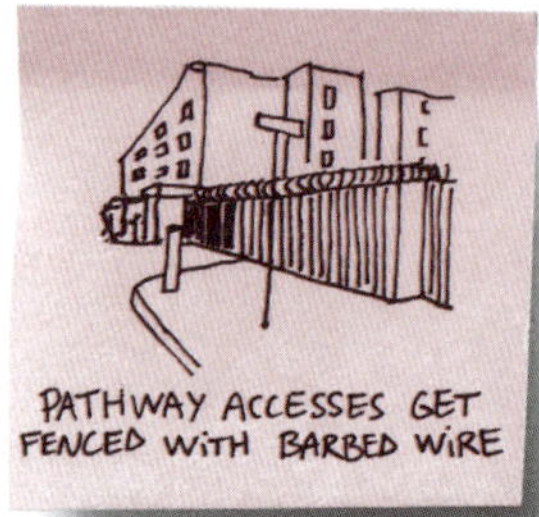
PATHWAY ACCESSES GET
FENCED WITH BARBED WIRE

NOOKS AND RESIDUAL
AREAS GET FENCED

THINGS ARE COVERED
AND HIDDEN FROM VIEW

ACCESSES GET FENCED
AND PERSONALIZED
WITH OBJECTS

FOUNTAINS ARE
ABANDONED AND FENCED

PARKING LOTS
GET FENCED

ANY NOOK OR CORNER
OF FREE SPACE
IS FENCED

Gates define limits and fragment the landscape, turning it into passageways and corridors that push social life out of public areas.

Gates in HU are "untouchable," they privatize space, and cannot be challenged.

Most people associate a gate with security, nonetheless they generate exactly the opposite: they block visibility, serve as a hideaway for robbers and often turn into junkyards.

Gates fragment common areas, interrupt circulation flows, degenerate into underused spaces; however, they are the constant in the context of HU.

Habitability refers to a space's capacity to welcome and engage people on a human scale in everyday routines. It is intimately linked to the atmospheres generated by the choice and use of construction materials, design proportions, turning it into a harmonious space.

The growth of Mexico, poverty and inequality, have all drastically increased. Therefore, it is not the responsibility of the architect alone, but of managers, officials and citizens to work together to solve the problems of habitability and generate meaning of common unity.

HABITABILITY

H

Habitability is not solely about sheltering daily habits, but also about nourishing meaning and a state of wellbeing.

Habitability implies promoting the use of space regardless of its function; it is what makes an area thoughtful.

Habits define the ultimate use of space. A pattern comes to be by repetition of an action generating a lifestyle, a way of being.

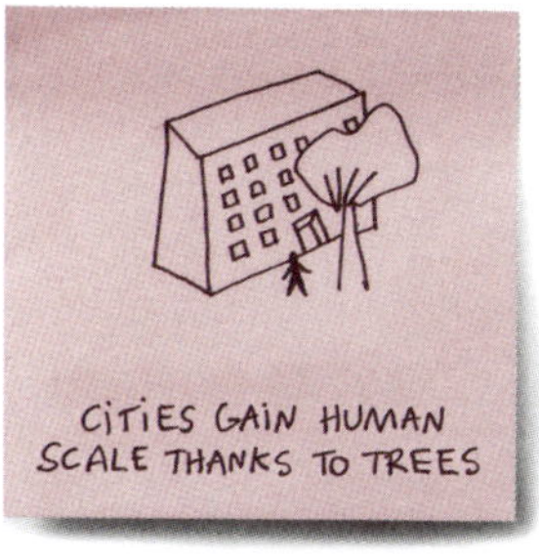

SHRINES HAVE A PLACE
OF THEIR OWN IN
EVERY HU

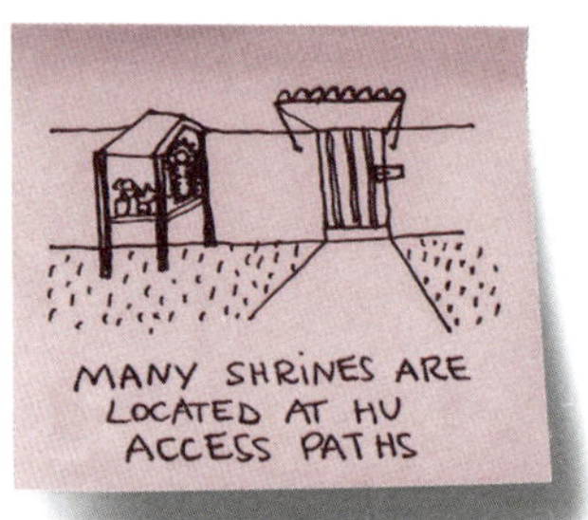
MANY SHRINES ARE
LOCATED AT HU
ACCESS PATHS

IDENTITY

I

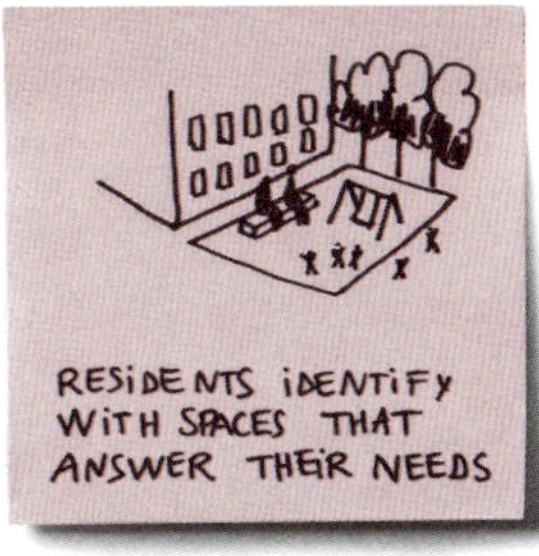

Architecture seeks congruence with the identity of a place.

The community maintains the common space when it identifies and appropriates it.

The shape and spatial distribution of the HU, as well as the relation and interpretations that the inhabitants make of their public spaces, have lost identity, and therefore, the meaning of community.

After being implemented, if a design remains active, a site acquires its own identity. The ultimate result of "making a place" is connecting life with space.

Common-Unity: Housing Unit public space project by REA, Azcapotzalco, Mexico City, 2015–2016

The most significant drawback faced by people living in informal settlements is not the lack of resources, but the disengagement from political representation; the shortage of professional assistance; scarcity of open technologies: alienation from the public realm.

INFORMALITY

Almost half of Mexico City is self-built.

Informal daily trade brings all kinds of products into HU, from music to sewing kits.

Finding opportunities in the informal use of space is critical to expand and re-signify common areas efficiently.

Informality makes the city an affordable venture; and unlike alienated suburbia, social capital and entrepreneurship thrive on it. People do not take the city for granted; they build it daily in organic ways.

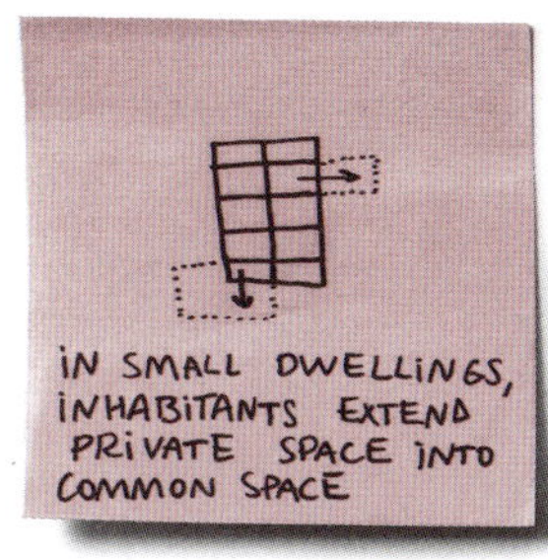

Informal constructions in front of Jasmin Housing Unit, Rinconada de los Reyes Crisantemo, Mexico City, 2017

"The internal is organic.

The interior, physical.

The intimate, ethical.

The intrinsic, philosophical.

The internal is studied.

The interior is registered.

The intimate is felt.

The intrinsic is explained."

Roque Barcia.

INTERIOR

The dimensions of the interior spaces in the HU are reduced, for this reason, the public spaces become a habitable extension.

Although the interior spaces are small, if the design of the common space is convenient, the internal dimension become less critical.

In several HU, public spaces become interior courtyards.

A combination of room divisions transforms a space and even blurs the boundaries between the inside and the outside in an HU.

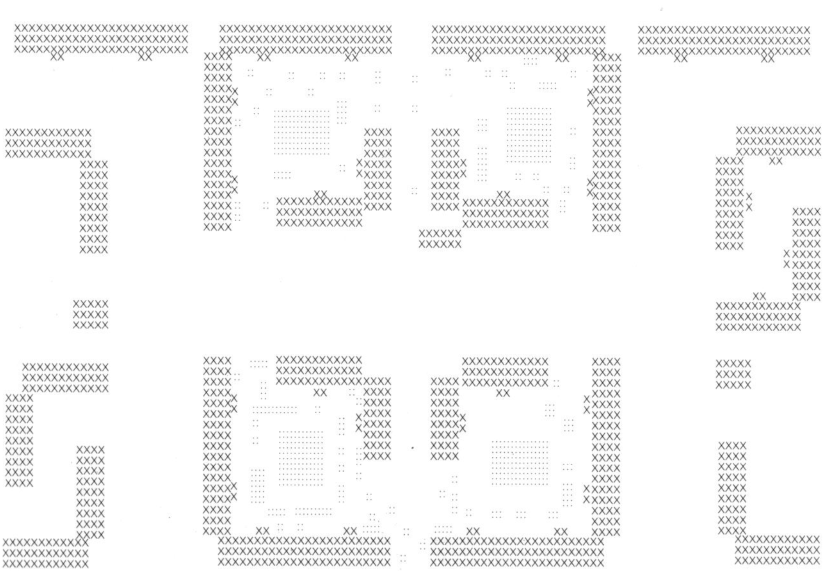

Common-Unity: Housing Unit public space project by REA, Azcapotzalco, Mexico City, 2015–2016

One strategy for people to stop throwing garbage is to put up an altar. We have confirmed that transformed dumps become sacred places that people clean and respect.

In Mexico, in general, there is no culture around garbage: people throw it away, it is not sorted out, and plastic bags with trash become a kind of magnet for people to leave more garbage.

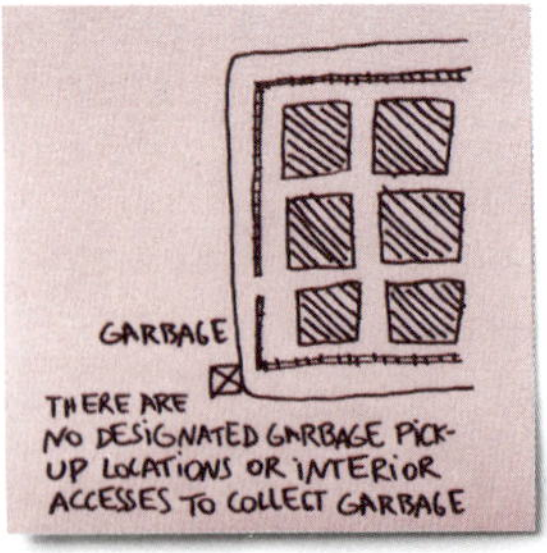

JUNK

One of the questions that still have no answer is, how to solve the problem of junk in the HU?

Some open spaces, destined to green areas, become residual spaces: garbage dumps or private property of the closest neighbor, affect the quality of life of the inhabitant as well as the environment.

In the garbage dumps of the public areas, all kinds of waste coexist, which, like a bottomless pit, attracts more trash that no one can or wants to remove.

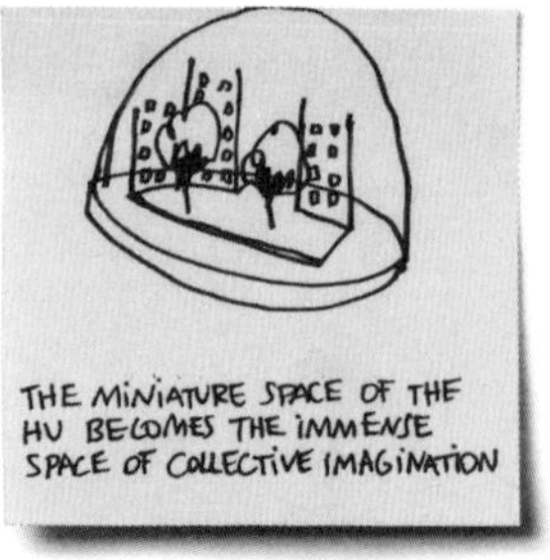

"All children,

as long as they still live in the mystery,

are continuously occupied in their souls

with the only thing that is important,

which is themselves

and their enigmatic relationship with the world

around them."

Herman Hesse

Any object a kid may find turns into a play element.

A child and teen-friendly city guarantee a city´s future.

The child does not need elements that reproduce an imaginary; he creates it with physical, mental, emotional and social experiences, that only a free space allows.

With HU rehabilitation, children that used to roam endlessly around the streets, now have a place to be, to go to, and to play in.

Kids and teens are vulnerable groups that most benefit from informal learning spaces.

As children are a sector of the population capable of making changes in society, they need stimulating spaces to develop creativity.

"Childhood is destiny." Children are a reflection of the city; their habitat is a reflection of their behavior.

Fresnillo Playground: Housing Unit public space project by REA, Fresnillo, Zacatecas, 2017

a
b
c
d
e
f
g
h
i
j
k
l
m
n
o
p
q
r
s
t
u
v
w
x
y
z

LEARN

Learning is acquiring knowledge. To apprehend is to conceive species of spaces through experience to be fixed in memory.

Games are transformed into working methods that allow visualizing the histories and routes of the inhabitants of the HU.

The reading spaces we design in the HU are linked to teaching, learning, and knowledge.

With imagination, the world is built.

The experience of reading, play, coexistence and exchange are the foundation of ideas, that is, the pure knowledge of human understanding.

Research looks for traces, prints, signs, and vestiges. It is the work of a detective: to recollect information to learn about the role of people in the space they inhabit.

Architecture is a collective practice involving many forces; learning to manage them beyond oneself is part of the trade.

lla
osa
un amigo
BIC

Common-Unity: Housing Unit public space project by REA, Azcapotzalco, Mexico City, 2015–2016

LARGE COMMON AREAS
NEED SHADE AND
LIGHTING

A ROPE WITH LAMPS
LIGHTS UP PUBLIC SPACE

LIGHT

Landscapes of light and sound overlap during days and seasons. In general, the function of space enables us to dwell in the present.

Light in architecture generates interior and exterior atmospheres that produce a state of well-being.

Light can make objects visible in their vertical and horizontal dimensions, as well as in their distances to generate games of light and shadow.

Clarity is the intrinsic quality of light.

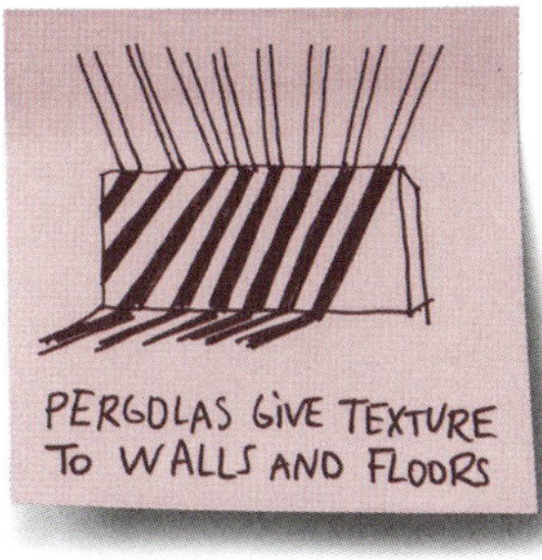

Common-Unity: Housing Unit public space project by REA, Azcapotzalco, Mexico City, 2015–2016

Drawing a line becomes a frontier, creates a limit, where people reorganize and modify their interactions inside and outside in such a boundary.

LIMIT

To inhabit the border or limit as space where to carry out actions. The limit is an area, a habitable border, a border without lines where intersection possibilities exist.

THE QUALITY OF A
MATERIAL CAN PRODUCE
WELLBEING OR DISCOMFORT

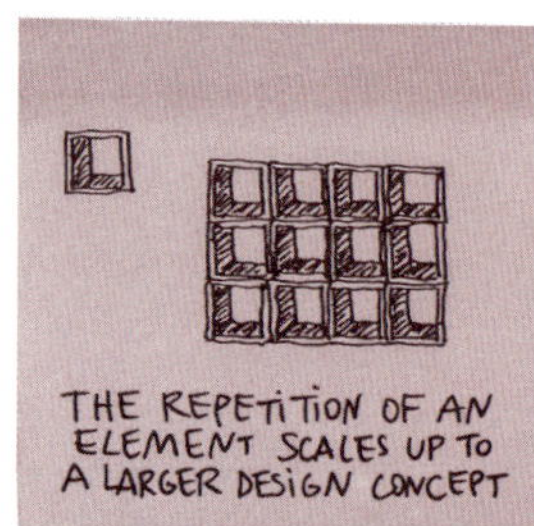
THE REPETITION OF AN
ELEMENT SCALES UP TO
A LARGER DESIGN CONCEPT

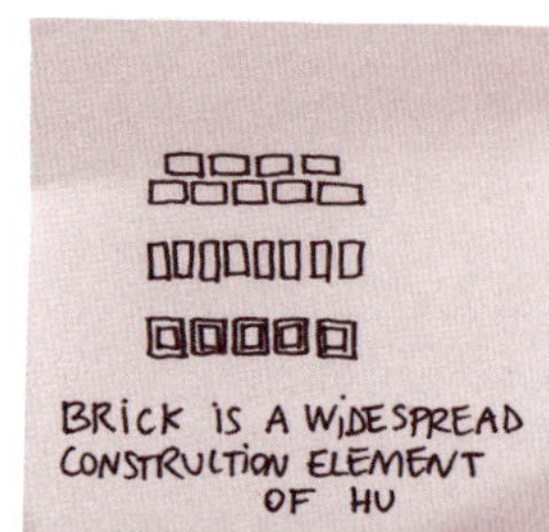
BRICK IS A WIDESPREAD
CONSTRUCTION ELEMENT
OF HU

MATERIALITY

M

Materiality defines a space's character. It modulates atmospheres and experience by establishing patterns, rhythms, visual warmth and shades of color.

Materials have bio-climatic properties, their combination and sourcing can lower carbon foot-prints and solve environment issues.

In the HU, we re-signify materials.

Material design can make a difference between livable spaces and wastelands.

Landscape and nature are real constituents of a palette of materials.

Hand-crafted materials add a human imprint to any space, interlacing cultural and historical values. Haptic spatial experiences show us that the skin is also capable of "seeing."

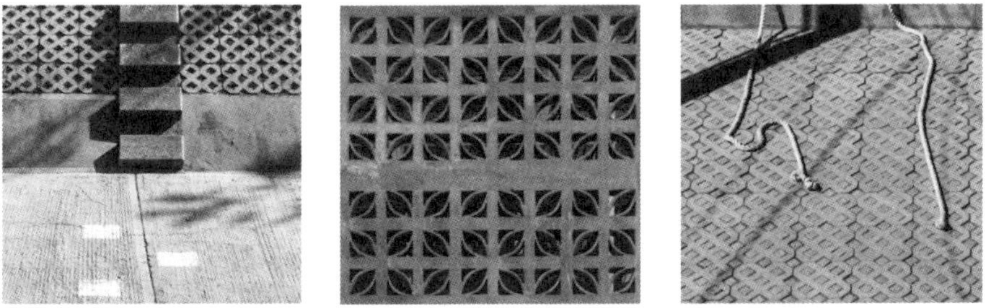

Common-Unity, Court, Fresnillo Playground: details

Exploring new schemes to represent space is a critical thinking exercise; the interpretation of a project cannot be disassociated from its

representation.

Our approach has a multi-sensory understanding of space;

we often experiment with new materials, or re-signify common elements by placing the accent on singular formal methodologies of building systems.

METHODOLOGY

An interdisciplinary approach allows people to borrow tools and knowledge from other professional practices.

We redraw continuously to get a closer look at the real,
picking up d
e
t
a
i
l
s that are crucial in transforming reality.

SE MAPEAN LAS EXPERIENCIAS DE LOS HABITANTES PARA CONOCER SU PERCEPCIÓN
EL ESPACIO ABIERTO RESPONDE A NUMEROSAS NECESIDADES Y USOS
LAS VENTANAS SE DECORAN
EDIFICIO
UN MURETE SIRVE PARA COLOCAR VARIOS ELEMENTOS
LOS EDIFICIOS COMPONEN EL ESPACIO VACÍO Y COMÚN
UN TEJIDO SOCIAL SE PUEDE CONSTRUIR A PARTIR DE SITUACIONES
LAS COLUMNAS SIRVEN COMO SOPORTES DE DIVERSOS USOS
LOS OBJETOS COMPONEN EL ESPACIO
LOS ARQUITECTOS RECOLECTAN INFORMACIÓN VALIOSA
EL ESPACIO ABIERTO Y EL ESPACIO CONSTRUIDO ESTÁN INTERCONECTADOS
EL JUEGO DE ILUSIÓN ÓPTICA CAMBIA LA PERCEPCIÓN DE UNA BARRERA
LAS ESQUINAS PEQUEÑAS RESIDUALES TAMBIÉN SE ENREJAN
REPARAR NO ES CAMBIAR
LOS HUECOS DE LAS ESCALERAS SE CONVIERTEN EN COMEDOR Y ESTAR
EL ESPACIO MINIATURA DE LAS UH, ES EL ESPACIO INMENSO DEL IMAGINARIO
LO ESTÉTICO PUEDE SER ECONÓMICO Y DE CALIDAD
EL PASTO EN LOS JUEGOS SE EROSIONA. SE INUNDA
LAS COSAS SE TAPAN Y CUBREN
CADA ESPACIO NECESITA UN HILO CONDUCTOR
EL ESPACIO COMÚN ES PARA CONOCER LA DIVERSIDAD
EL ESPACIO COMÚN ES TAMBIÉN ESPACIO DE COLGAR
LA PROXIMIDAD CREA INTERACCIÓN
UN ESPACIO VACÍO ENTRE DOS EDIFICIOS PUEDE OCUPARSE CON VARIOS USOS
EL ESPACIO ABIERTO SE CONSTRUYE CON, EN Y PARA EL TIEMPO
LOS KIT PERMITEN CREATIVIDAD
LOS HABITANTES COLOCAN ALTARES
LAS BICICLETAS SE TAPAN Y SE ESTACIONAN EN LOS PASILLOS
UN ESPACIO VACÍO SE PUEDE CONVERTIR EN PLAYGROUND
LOS GRAFITIS SON SÍMBOLOS DE FALTA DE INTEGRACIÓN DE LA JUVENTUD
LOS HABITANTES NECESITAN ESTACIONARSE
LOS CAJONES DE ESTACIONAMIENTO SE ENREJAN
LOS ESPACIOS COMUNES GRANDES NECESITAN SOMBRA Y MÁS ILUMINACIÓN
DONDE SE PUEDE HACER COMERCIO, SE HACE
HAY ELEMENTOS MOVIBLES Y OTROS NO
LOS ACCESOS SE ENREJAN Y SE COLOCAN PÚAS
EL ÉXITO DE UN PROYECTO NO DEPENDE DE SU COSTO
EXISTEN VARIOS TIPOS DE ESPACIOS VERDES PEQUEÑOS
EL KIT FACILITA LA OBRA
ESPACIOS VERDES CONTENIDOS SE VUELVEN BASUREROS
UN TECHO EN UN ACCESO PERMITE PROTEGERSE DE LA LLUVIA
CONDUCIR EL AGUA PARA INFILTRARLA
LOS TRONCOS TAMBIÉN DELIMITAN ESPACIOS
CADA HABITANTE ES ÚNICO
SE AÑADEN ESCALERAS A LA VENTANA
ENTENDER UN LUGAR ES ESCUCHAR A LA GENTE
UN MURO QUE SEPARA SE TRANSFORMA POR UN TECHO QUE UNE
EL SONIDO DE LOS AMBULANTES MARCA EL TIEMPO DE LA UH
LA SEÑALIZACIÓN AYUDA A UBICAR
LA GENTE CAMINA DERECHO Y BUSCA EL CAMINO MÁS CORTO
LA PEQUEÑA UH ES LA ESCALA DEL NIÑO
UN ELEMENTO DE 40-40 CON CIERTO ESPESOR SIRVE DE BANCA
CIUDAD
LOS AUTOS BLOQUEAN LA BANQUETA Y LA ENTRADA A LA UH
UN ÁRBOL CAMBIA MUCHO
UN CRUCE ENTRE TALUDES PUEDE TENER PROGRAMA
EN MÉXICO, HAY UNA TEMPORADA DE LLUVIAS Y LA CIUDAD SE INUNDA
SE RECOLECTA EL AGUA PLUVIAL PEDALEANDO EN UNA BICIMÁQUINA
UN MURO PUEDE TENER DOBLE USO: COMERCIO
LOS KIT PERMITEN BAJOS COSTOS
CUALQUIER ESQUINA Y RINCÓN ABIERTO SE ENREJA
EL ESPACIO COMÚN ES ESPACIO PEATONAL EN LA CIUDAD DEL AUTOMÓVIL
LAS MACETAS DELIMITAN ESPACIOS
UN MURO SE UTILIZA COMO MEDIO DE COMUNICACIÓN
LOS HABITANTES ABANDONAN SUS COSAS Y ESTAS PERMANECEN
LOS AMBULANTES MARCAN TIEMPO
UN EDIFICIO TAMBIÉN PUEDE TENER PROGRAMAS PÚBLICOS
LA ARQUITECTURA ES UN JUEGO DE ESCALA DE LO GRANDE A LO MICRO
LAS PLANTAS TIENEN UN VOLUMEN INVISIBLE: LAS RAÍCES
UNA RAMPA ES UN ELEMENTO INCLUYENTE
SE AUMENTAN LOS ESPACIOS SACANDO LAS VENTANAS
EN VIVIENDAS PEQUEÑAS LOS HABITANTES EXTIENDEN SU ESPACIO PRIVADO AL ESPACIO COMÚN
CONCIERTOS
LOS ESPACIOS COMUNES ERAN LOS ESPACIOS RESULTANTES Y NO COMPONENTES ESTRUCTURALES
EL DESNIVEL SE PUEDE APROVECHAR PARA DEPORTE
EL PLAYGROUND PUEDE TENER VARIOS USOS
LOS ELEMENTOS SENCILLOS HACEN GRANDES JUEGOS
EL ESPACIO Y EL TIEMPO SE COMPARTEN
LOS HABITANTES CONVIERTEN LO PÚBLICO EN PRIVADO
LAS CELOSÍAS SON ELEMENTOS PARA OBSERVAR SIN SER OBSERVADO
PONER UN MOBILIARIO NO ES DAR UN USO
UN TALUD CON PENDIENTE ES UN ESPACIO PARA PROPONER JUEGOS
LA TRANSFORMACIÓN DEL ESPACIO PUEDE SER UN MOMENTO LÚDICO
EL LÍMITE PUEDE SER UN CAMBIO EN EL PISO
LA BANQUETA TAMBIÉN LA OCUPAN LOS AUTOS
LOS HABITANTES FORMAN REDES.
EL PLAYGROUND TIENE DIFERENTES ESCALAS
CUARTO
LAS HOJAS NO SON BASURA
LOS ESPACIOS ABIERTOS NECESITAN DISTINTOS NIVELES DE MANTENIMIENTO
BAILE
EL MÓDULO
EL ESPACIO VERTICAL

LOS HABITANTES SE IDENTIFICAN CON UN ESPACIO QUE RESPONDE A SUS NECESIDADES
LAS MOTOS Y BICIS BLOQUEAN LOS ACCESOS A LAS UH
UNA ESQUINA ABIERTA E ILUMINADA ES UN LUGAR DE ENCUENTRO
LOS REGISTROS SE CONVIERTEN EN BASUREROS
UNA LÍNEA GENERA ESPACIO
LOS ÁRBOLES TIENEN VALOR Y TRAEN OXÍGENO
ENTRE COLUMNAS SE GENERA ESPACIO
LOS ESPACIOS COMUNES SON VERTICALES Y HORIZONTALES
LA BANQUETA SE OCUPA PARA DEJAR BASURA
UN ESPACIO ABIERTO CONCURRIDO TIENE MENOS PROBLEMAS QUE UNO INVISIBLE
AUNQUE NOS MOVEMOS CON EL, EL CARRO SIEMPRE ES UN LÍMITE
UN ESPACIO VERDE NECESITA MANTENIMIENTO
LA CIUDAD ES UNA SERIE DE PATRONES
LA GENTE SE SIENTA CON LA ESPALDA PROTEGIDA
LAS SITUACIONES CAMBIAN EL ESPACIO
EL COMERCIO SE EXTIENDE INFINITAMENTE
LA CIUDAD TIEMBLA Y LOS PISOS LISOS SE ROMPEN
LA CELOSÍA ES UN ELEMENTO COMÚN EN LAS UH
DEJAR ESPACIO ENTRE LOS PAVIMENTOS PERMITE A LA VEGETACIÓN CRECER Y AL AGUA PASAR
UN TALUD SIRVE PARA MUCHOS OTROS USOS
UN MURO SE UTILIZA PARA PROYECTAR PELÍCULAS
EL ESPACIO PUEDE SUGERIR USOS
A LOS EDIFICIOS SE LES AÑADEN PRÓTESIS
LOS OBJETOS SON PRUEBAS DE UNA APROPIACIÓN
LOS ACCESOS SE LLENAN DE COMERCIOS
LA CIRCULACIÓN GENERA ESPACIO
EL JUEGO PUEDE SER DEPORTE
LAS LONAS SON UN ELEMENTO MUY USADO
LOS TALUDES, MURETES Y LOS ÁRBOLES GENERAN PASEOS
CON SUS GESTICULACIONES, UN MIMO GENERA ESPACIO
TALUD
LOS ESPACIOS GRANDES SIN SOMBRA Y LLENOS DE CARROS NO SON AMIGABLES
LAS PLANTAS BAJAS PUEDEN SER ESPACIOS COMUNES CUANDO LLUEVE
CRUZAR
INSTITUCIÓN
INFONAVIT
HABITANTE
CONSTRUCCIÓN
ARQUITECTO
LOS BALCONES SE LLENAN DE OBJETOS
LAS FACHADAS SE CUBREN CON MERCANCÍA
EL PLAYGROUND ACOMPAÑA LA CIUDAD AMIGABLE
LOS TRONCOS TAMBIÉN SIRVEN COMO BANCAS
CADA HABITANTE TIENE COMPETENCIAS
PASEAR
UN ÁRBOL APROVECHA EL ESPACIO VERTICAL SIN OCUPAR MUCHO EL PISO
LAS FUENTES SE ABANDONAN Y SE ENREJAN
LAS AZOTEAS TIENEN VARIOS USOS
LOS ACCESOS SE ENREJAN Y SE PERSONALIZAN CON OBJETOS
SE ADORNAN ESTRUCTURAS COMO CAPILLAS
UNA GUARNICIÓN SE VUELVE BANCA
ES IMPORTANTE TENER SEÑALIZACIÓN PARA UBICARSE EN LAS UH
LOS PATIOS INTERIORES SON TAMBIÉN TENDEDEROS
UNA BODEGA ABANDONADA EN LA BANQUETA PUEDE OCUPARSE CON OTROS USOS
UNA ACCIÓN EFÍMERA PUEDE MODIFICAR EL USO DE UN ESPACIO
UN MURO TIENE GRAN POTENCIAL DE SER USADO
LOS ESCALONES SON FUENTE DE JUEGOS
UNA BANCA NO SIEMPRE SIRVE PARA SENTARSE
EL ÁRBOL GENERA ESCALA HUMANA
OBJETO
CUALQUIER ESQUINA SIRVE COMO TENDEDERO
LA CIUDAD ES UNA SERIE DE PATRONES
UN ÁRBOL CORTADO PUEDE SER UN BANCO
LOS ALTARES EXISTEN EN CADA UH Y CONSTRUYEN ESPACIOS
UNA FACHADA CON VENTANAS CUIDA AL ESPACIO COMÚN
LAS CELOSÍAS SE USAN COMO CONTENCIÓN DE LA VEGETACIÓN
DISEÑAR ESPACIOS PARA TODOS ES SER INCLUYENTE
LOS TALUDES Y PUENTES CREAN RECORRIDOS
EL BORDE TIENE UN ESPESOR
EL BORDE TAMBIÉN ES VOLUMEN
LAS RAÍCES DE LOS ÁRBOLES QUIEBRAN EL PAVIMENTO
COLGAR ROPA
EDIFICIOS CONECTADOS A LA RED DE TRANSPORTE HACEN CIUDAD
UN ELEMENTO DE CELOSÍA SE USA COMO PAVIMENTO
UN ESPACIO PEQUEÑO ENTRE MUROS ACABA SIENDO UN BASURERO
MERCADO
LA SOMBRA GENERA HABITABILIDAD
LOS ANIMALES TAMBIÉN SON HABITANTES DE LAS UH
LOS ELEMENTOS EXISTENTES OFRECEN POSIBILIDADES
HACER LUGAR GENERA COMUNIDAD
LA PEQUEÑA ESCALA ES MÁS AMABLE
LO QUE SE PUEDE SE ACUMULA
LA INTERIORIDAD TRAE INTIMIDAD
UNA REJA SE TRANSFORMA EN PÉRGOLA
LOS HABITANTES SE QUIEREN DISTINGUIR DE LOS DEMÁS
METER EL EXTERIOR

Many housing developments have turned into lifeless dormitory blocks, and such social depression is a significant factor that affects the value of real estate property.

MOBILITY

Constructing HU's far from the city centers has generated a severe problem of inequality due to long hours spent on commuting.

In Mexico City, people spend a daily average of two to three hours commuting, and close to 30% of their income is spent on transportation expenses.

People waste away their lives getting to places.

Displacement manages mobility and regulates time shifts in the use of spaces and networks.

San Pablo Xalpa Housing Unit, Azcapotzalco, Mexico City, 2016

MODULAR

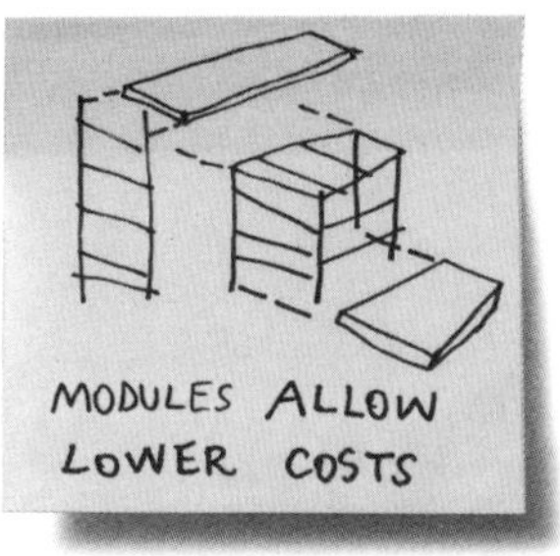

A module introduces flexibility; its rhythm and repetition produce changes in its configuration.

A module is a piece or unit set of pieces that are repeated in any construction, to make it easier, regular and economical.

The module measures and gives dimensions to architectural proportions. A well-modulated public space invites to inhabit it and multiplies its functions.

The module modifies the factors that intervene in the design process of space to obtain different results.

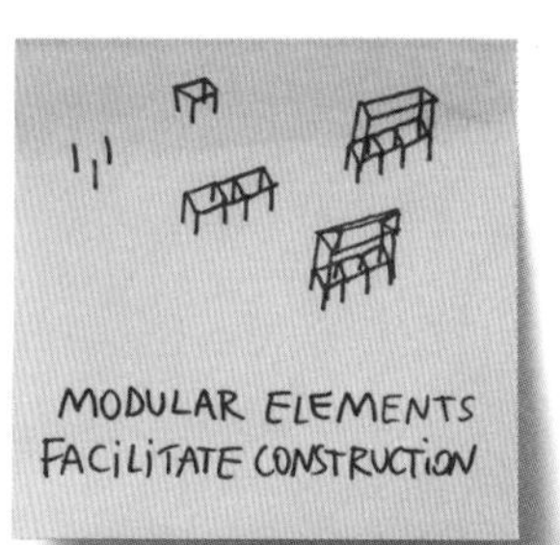

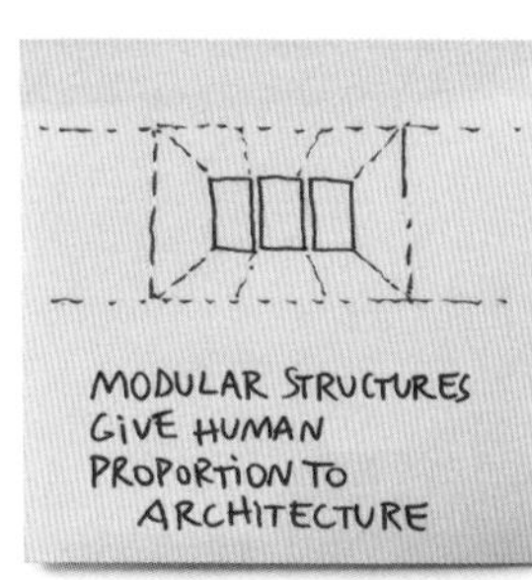

Common-Unity: Housing Unit public space project by REA, Azcapotzalco, Mexico City, 2015-2016

STUFF ABANDONED BY RESIDENTS IN COMMON AREAS STAYS AROUND

HU RAMPS HAVE INADEQUATELY ANGLED SLOPES

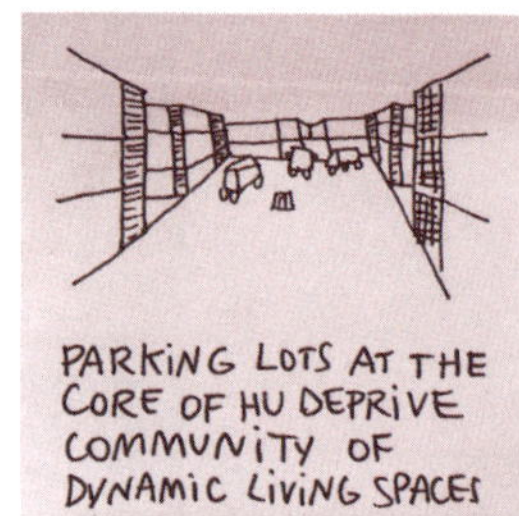
PARKING LOTS AT THE CORE OF HU DEPRIVE COMMUNITY OF DYNAMIC LIVING SPACES

PEOPLE KILL AND CUT UP TREES BECAUSE LEAF-SHEDDING IS PERCEIVED AS A PUBLIC NUISANCE

TURPENTINE CANS ARE PLACED INSIDE LIVING TREE TRUNKS TO DRY THEM UP

AN ABANDONED STOREROOM ON THE SIDEWALK SUGGESTS OTHER USES

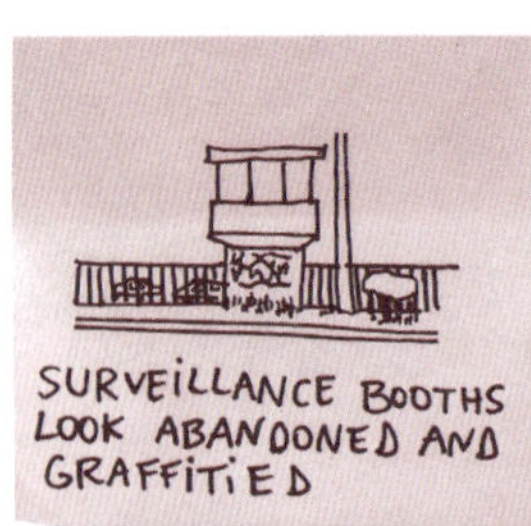
SURVEILLANCE BOOTHS LOOK ABANDONED AND GRAFFITIED

NEGLECT

N

Although 70% of what is built in Mexico are HU, up to 15-20% of them are regularly abandoned.

One of the reasons why people leave UH homes is that there are no suitable public services nearby: transportation, schools, hospitals, parks.

Public space in many HU´s usually deteriorates, is underutilized or abandoned, fenced and taken over for undesirable purposes. It rarely works as a space in which the community interacts for its benefit.

The public space in HU becomes a scale model of the urban public space. It reproduces the dynamics, flows and temporalities of the city: anomalies, extraordinary uses, and disuse, abandonment: a hybrid of overlapping programs and typological juxtapositions of indefinite normativity.

When there is no claim over space, neither visual nor physical, the area falls into disuse, deteriorating the quality of HU inhabitant's life.

place a life occupies in public space: belongings of a resident evicted from his apartment, camped permanently in the HU premises
Cobre y Aluminio Housing Unit, Mexico City, 2017

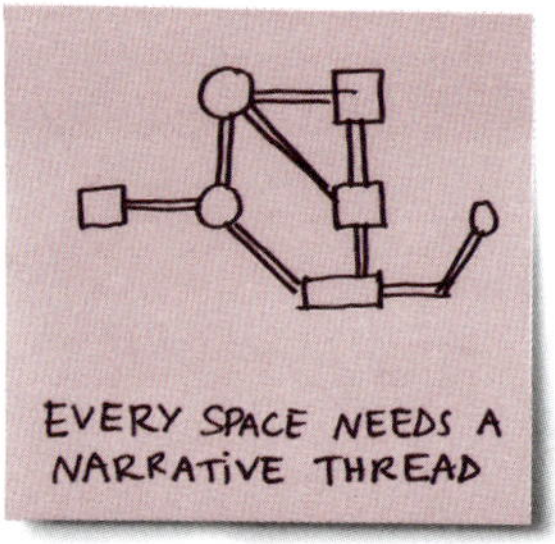
EVERY SPACE NEEDS A
NARRATIVE THREAD

NETWORK

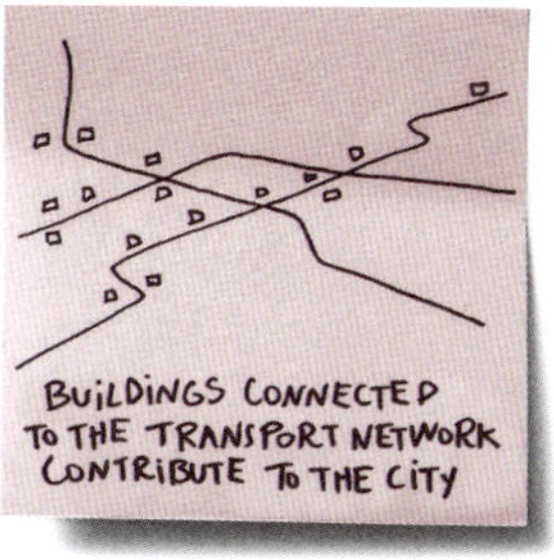

The multi-service centers at HU´s not only create a network of their own; they give a service to surrounding neighborhoods at street level. They interconnect the "underground city" to the "overground city."

The HU work on different layers and scales, they are a network of networks that could potentially increase people´s life quality and opportunities, therefore change the identity of the city itself.

The set of practices, atmospheres, networks, customs, and behaviors, which make a social group have a sense of place, materialize the common good in the public realm.

Specific functions of any HU projects are to create connectivity and permeability between the site and the city to produce networks of activities, pedestrian mobility, biological corridors, water, energy.

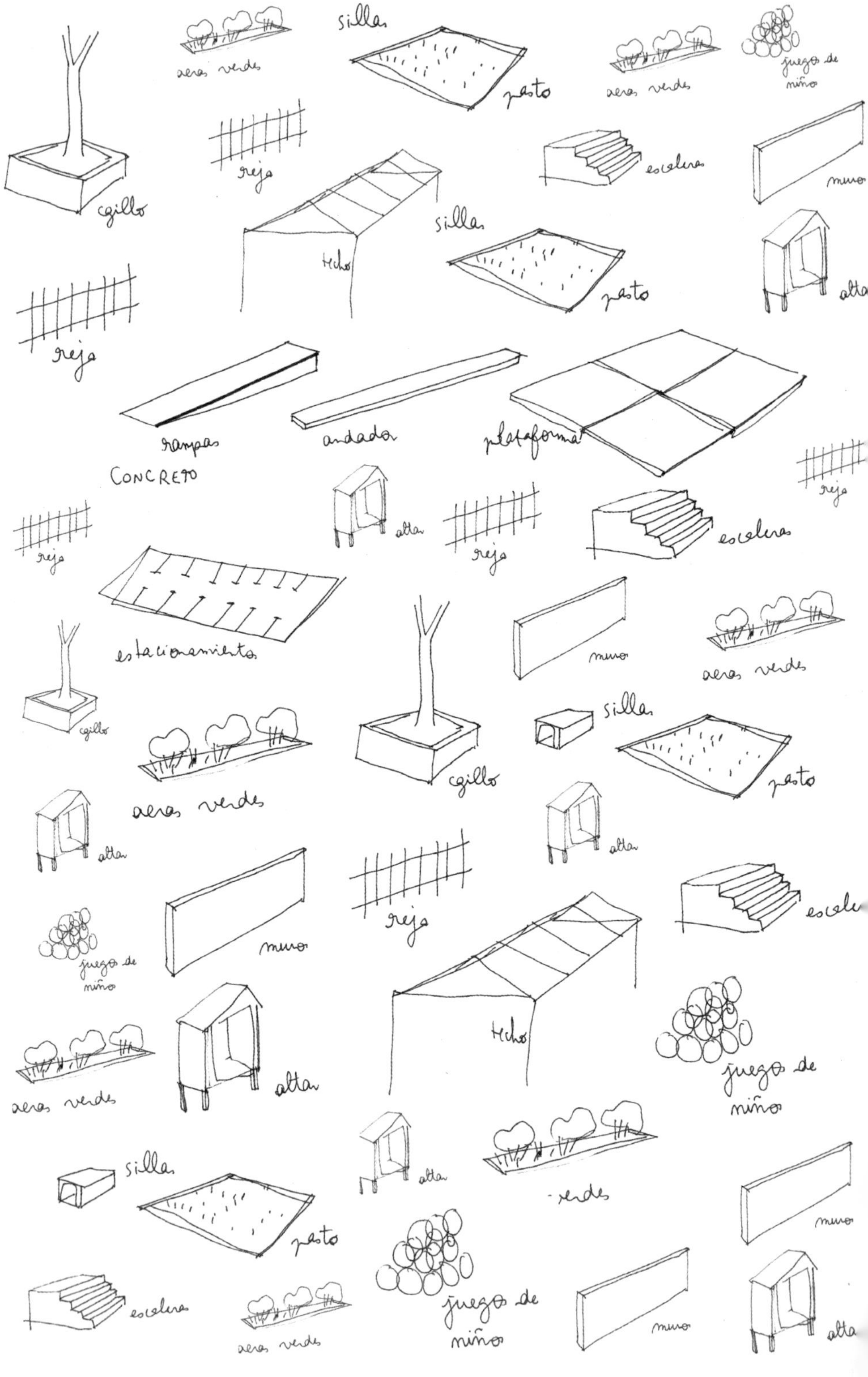

aeras verdes
sillas
pasto
aeras verdes
juegos de niños
rejas
techo
escaleras
muro
sillas
pasto
rejas
rampas
andador
plataforma
CONCRETO
rejas
rejas
escaleras
rejas
estacionamientos
muro
aeras verdes
sillas
pasto
aeras verdes
rejas
escaleras
muro
juegos de niños
techo
juegos de niños
aeras verdes
sillas
pasto
verdes
muro
escaleras
aeras verdes
juegos de niños
muro

OBJECTS

A drain, a mirror, a gallon water bottle, a funnel, a grill, a ladder, an antenna, a wooden crate, a door, a metal bottle-top, a tire, a window, are given new meaning as domestic objects, as urban elements, as live artifacts from recycled materials.

Within an HU, spatial typologies are studied, and different architectural elements are classified (things, objects, phenomena). The results are related to a collection of objects or subjects that can interact, for example, a group of individuals who share similar interests or form groups based on the same type of elements.

By observing patterns of objects along the different HU´s, we found innovative ways of looking at the urban scene.

PROXIMITY CREATES
INTERACTION

THE SPACE SUGGESTS
ITS OWN USES

UNDERSTANDING A
PLACE IS LISTENING TO
ITS PEOPLE

PLACE-MAKING
ACTIVATES COMMUNITY

PEOPLE

P

The added value of enabling people to understand and redefine their space is that they become aware of what they have.

Relationships are people's first shelter; without them they are homeless.

Neighborhood culture is a necessity for people, especially for newcomers; otherwise, the struggle to create a network opens the door to all sorts of conflicts.

Seeking the common good, empowering the community and facilitating communication, makes common ground possible, collective experiences build and reshape community relationships.

Place-making is a powerful approach to spatial production that enhances life quality and interconnects people.

Equitable architecture benefits children, seniors, young people, disabled people, men, and women, homosexuals, transsexuals, all kinds of people. If the public space ignores or excludes a sector, it becomes a structural discrimination. Social segregation's consequences are atrocious and silent: buried in everyday routines and spaces. As architects and urban designers, we can perpetuate or change this sort of problem.

Fresnillo Playground: Housing Unit public space project by REA, Fresnillo, Zacatecas, 2017

Plaza de Santa Ana Housing Unit, Cuauhtémoc, Mexico city, 2015

PERCEPTION

Change begins with a shift of perception.

Understanding the resources and essential needs of a site can change people´s perceptions of their habitat.

When people get together to re-design their HU; public perception of space changes in such a way that the need to remove fences becomes evident.

A single trace is able to build a kind of perception, memory and community.

Architects translate perception and movement into a gaze. A relation between the optic and the haptic appears.

Haptic refers to the phenomenological perception of sensations, distances, temperatures, textures, and routes; it means anything that generates an intimate notion of space.

The perception of inhabiting a space is not limited to its real scale, but to the perceived one.

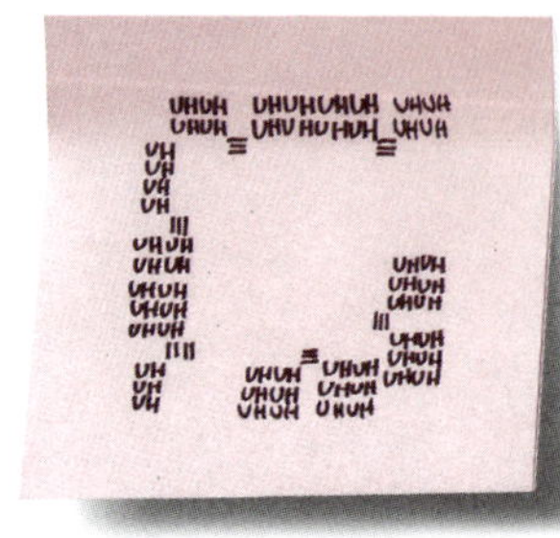

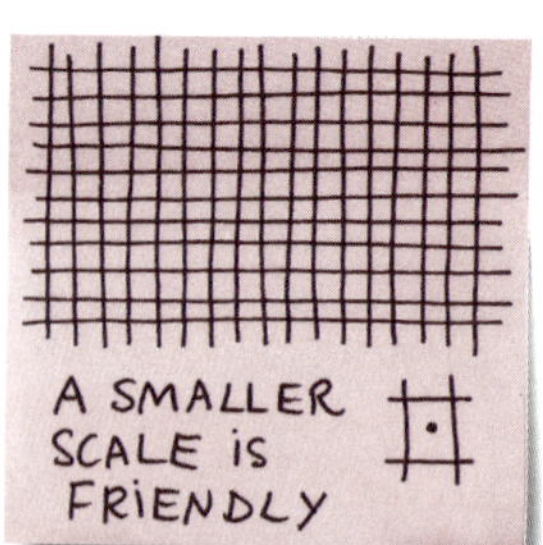

Place-making is a process more than a product. By approaching design as a process, we seek content in context.

Design that facilitates place-making builds a community.

Place-making is about building processes that enable meaningful connections between people and different species of spaces.

Small-scale projects admit ripple-effects on the larger scale when people get involved, not as consumers of space but as place-makers.

PLACE-MAKING

One of the architect's primary concerns is not just placing the displaced but rather creating a place for people to build meaningful relationships.

Place-making understands that the added value of architecture allows social constructions that lead to non-discriminatory economic growth and development opportunities.

Place-making as a spatial design concept reshapes community relationships by promoting new local culture. It implies a different approach to design: not envisioning it as a product or master plan, but as a process which takes place in several stages; as a working method, with different tactical approaches that manage not only spatial organization but also temporal uses of space.

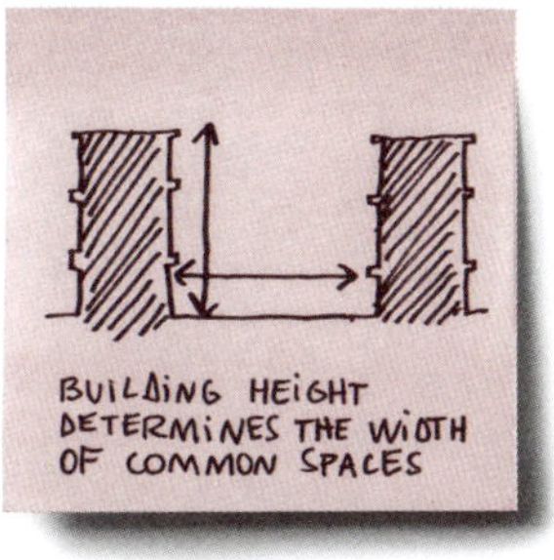

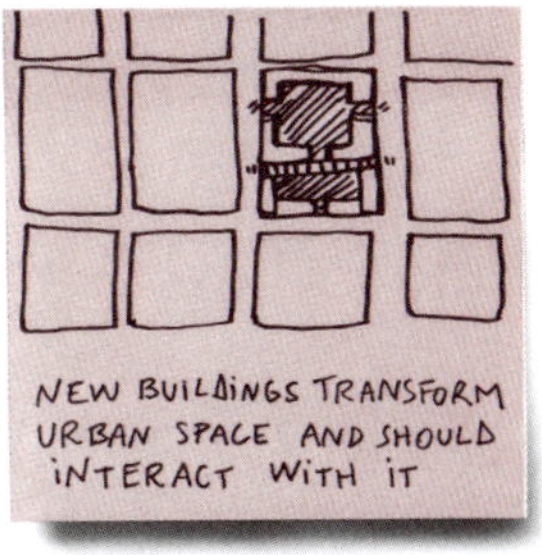

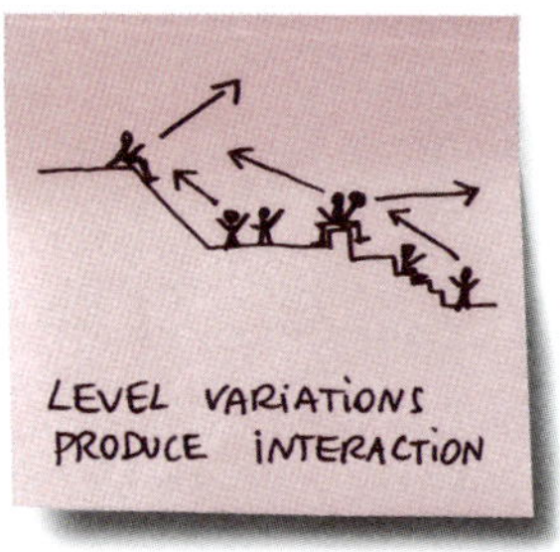

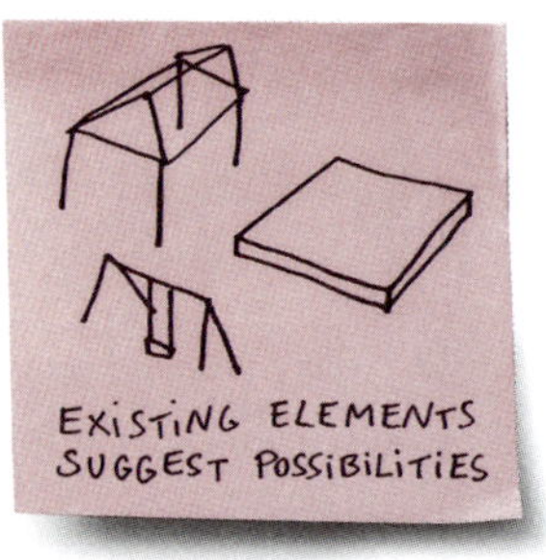

Playgrounds and youth hangouts are essential in bringing a community together.

Children and teenagers are vulnerable segments of the population that should be granted as many places for learning as possible. They are a crucial component of social integration rehabilitation.

Crossing paths are more than just a bridge; they are playgrounds in themselves; shaded spaces where people gather, a multifunctional area well illuminated by night to lead the way.

We find apparently derelict structures, like staircases going nowhere, and realize that skateboarders consider them "A skater's paradise." So, instead of demolishing, we enhance the place with guardrails, fun boxes, and ramps and add skater culture to the park's appeal.

PLAYGROUND

We transform underused areas into user-friendly functional playgrounds.

We see children sliding on rain gutters; we then transform an underused area into a functional playground accessible to everyone.

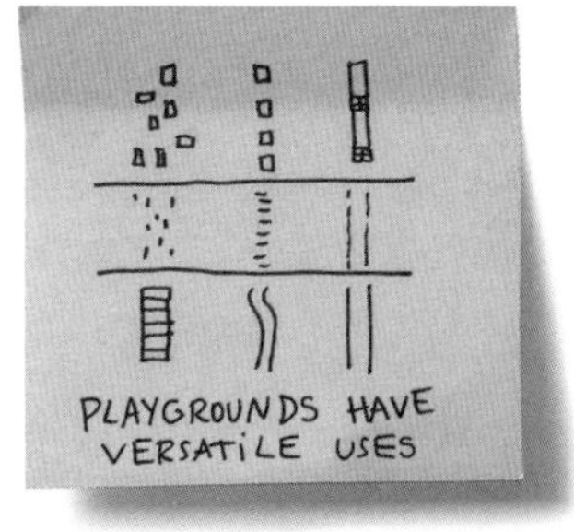

Fresnillo Playground: Housing Unit public space project by REA, Fresnillo, Zacatecas, 2017

Permeable pavement design for public areas is necessary to avoid flooding.

The porosity of the materials (ado-concrete, eco-concrete, lattices) allows the permeability of water and vegetation growth.

"'Poro' derives from the Greek root `passage´. Porosity, like any medium, allows transit from one stage to another. The porosity `crosses´ a limit and promotes a permanent state of many repercussions, only possible thanks to the continuous connection between the various points that make up a whole.

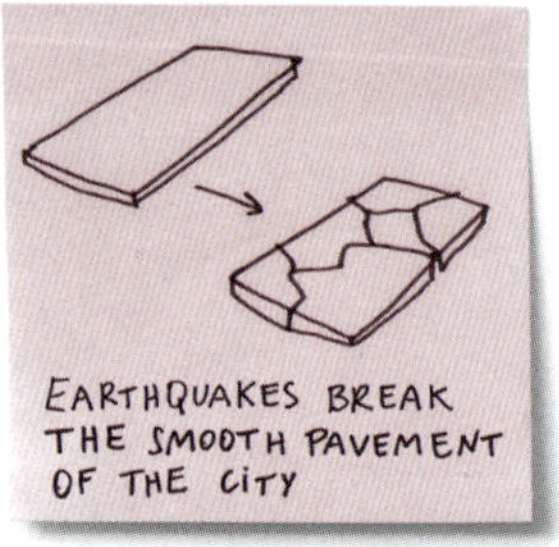

Porous architecture inhabits the border, makes the boundary a comfortable place, a state where porous relations become potential, where complexity grows present, converting the limit into a porous membrane."

Hammerly, Ma. Constance - Sarubi, Indiana - Sikh, Maria Paulina.

POROSITY

The notion of porosity refers to the space between solid elements, as well as the capacity of absorption of the soil to find a balance between hard (concrete) and porous surfaces (earth, vegetation).

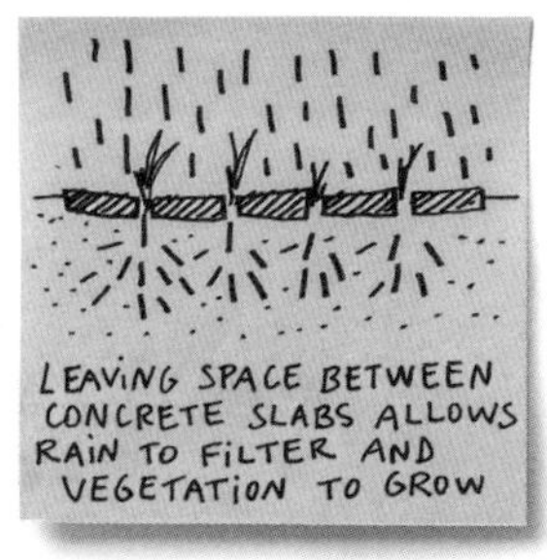

? ? ? ? ? ? ? ?
? ? ? ? ? ? ? ?
? ? ? ? ? ? ? ?
? ? ? ? ? ? ? ?
? ? ? ? ? ? ? ?
? ? ? ? ? ? ? ?
? ? ? ? ? ? ? ?
? ? ? ? ? ? ? ?
? ? ? ? ? ? ? ?

We approach design through different work logics: looking for an opportunity where others only see obstacles or bad habits. Since people encode everyday uses of space into habits, routines become second nature. By upholding what we call an active gaze, we learn to listen and perceive problems that others become accustomed to disregarding. Changing daily ways enable us to create and design more humane and habitable spaces; furthermore, allowing ourselves to ask questions as follows: In a world of limited time and resources, what is worth designing?

¿ ¿
¿ ¿
¿ ¿
¿ ¿
¿ ¿
¿ ¿
¿ ¿
¿ ¿
¿ ¿

QUERY ?

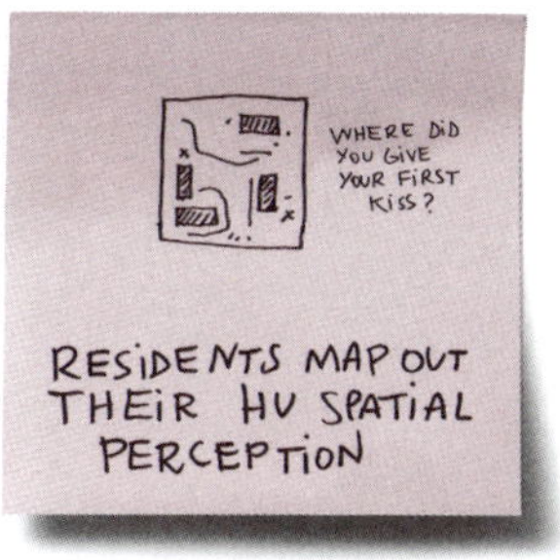

By implementing map-out-queries to HU habitants, we obtain and draw essential data about the specific usages of space, appealing to inhabitants' memories and emotions rather than to their rational selves.

Scientific inquiry has often led us outside the field of architecture into other disciplines in search of alternative, more powerful tools to sieve, shape and compile information about spatial perception. Our pursuits emphasize the design process itself as a language that needs to be probed by its epistemological and phenomenological effects.

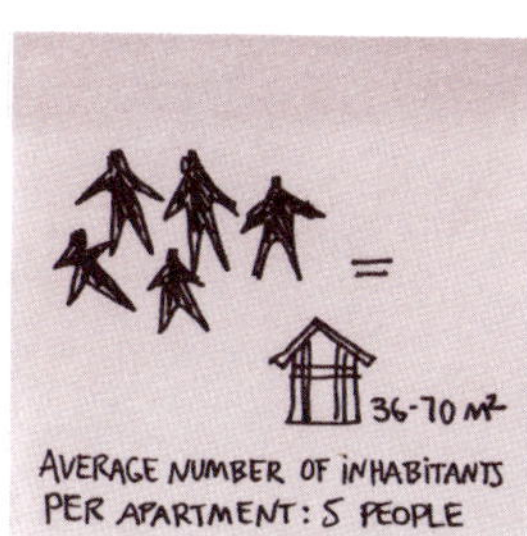

Fresnillo Playground: Housing Unit public space project by REA, Fresnillo, Zacatecas, 2017

Common-Unity: Housing Unit public space project by REA, Azcapotzalco, Mexico City, 2015-2016

/\ /\
\/ \/
/\ /\
\/ \/
/\ /\
\/ \/
/\ /\
\/ \/
/\ /\
\/ \/
/\ /\
\/ \/
/\ /\
\/ \/
/\ /\
\/ \/
/\ /\
\/ \/
/\ /\
\/ \/
/\ /\
\/ \/
/\ /\
\/ \/
/\ /\
\/ \/
/\ /\
\/ \/
/\ /\
\/ \/
/\ /\
\/ \/
/\ /\
\/ \/
/\ /\
\/ \/
/\ /\
\/ \/
/\ /\
\/ \/
/\ /\
\/ \/
/\ /\
\/ \/
/\ /\
\/ \/
/\ /\
\/ \/
/\ /\
\/ \/
/\ /\
\/ \/
/\ /\
\/ \/
/\ /\
\/ \/
/\ /\
\/ \/
/\ /\
\/ \/
/\ /\
\/ \/
/\ /\
\/ \/
/\ /\
\/ \/
/\ /\
\/ \/
/\ /\
\/ \/
/\ /\
\/ \/
/\ /\
\/ \/
/\ /\
\/ \/
/\ /\
\/ \/
/\ /\
\/ \/
/\ /\

RESIGNIFY

R

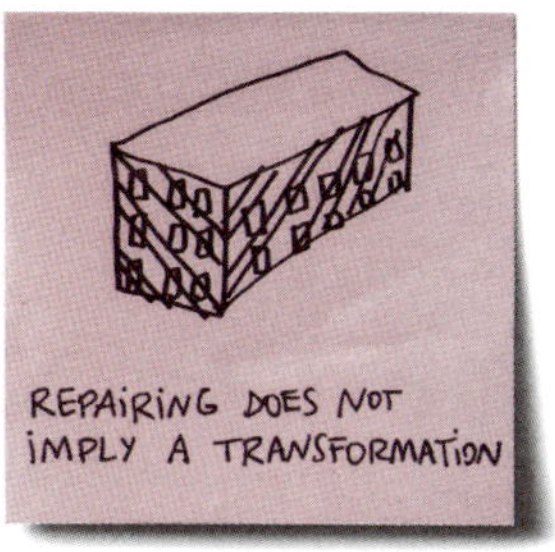

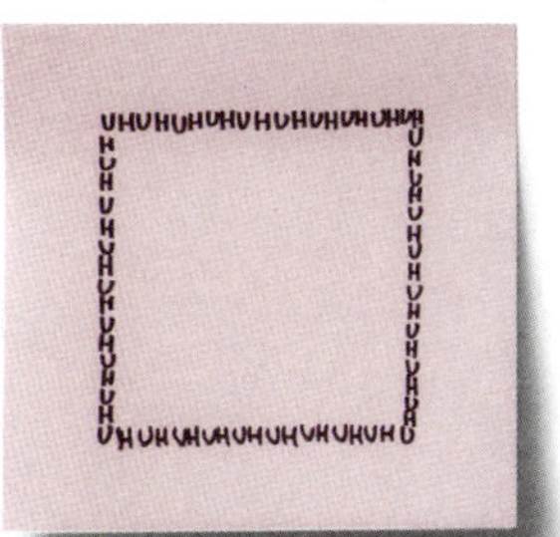

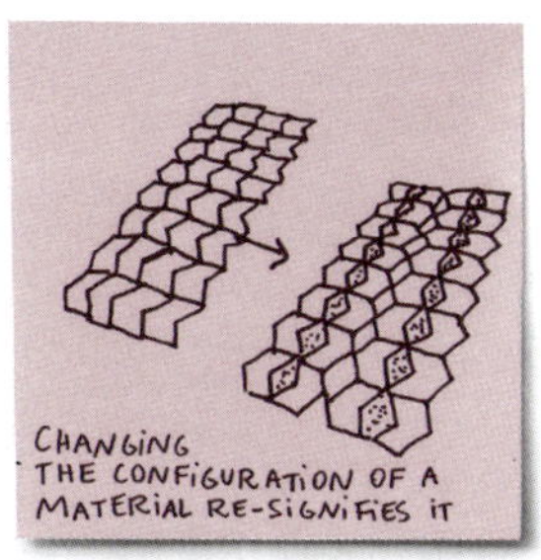

We developed an integral low-cost improvement of public space using simple materials, which we re-signified to speak a new language.

Representation in architectural design is not only a medium of conveying meaningful narratives of space but also of re-signifying our connections to space.

Observations, findings, insights, tactics and design solutions to intervene public space in HU are re-signified by our post-its that reveal the "making potential" behind our design process.

The post-it format has allowed us to encode a kind of visual aphorism that summarizes the principles for public space development in housing units.

Common-Unity: Housing Unit public space project by REA, Azcapotzalco, Mexico City, 2015–2016

All architecture is political. We build and design under contextualized normativity and legal constraints that reflect urban policies. We become political as we build in or for the polis, the city. Everyday decisions make a city; allowing us to read in daily spaces the legislative priorities of our society.

Architecture has the power to shape public behavior because, more than laying bricks, it lays the founding principles of public and social exchange. Architectural design has always been a socio-political activity to educate behavior.

As architects, we shape the political vision of the city's significant stakeholders by making them aware of the human aspects enabled by functional, striking design. The city we seek to create is one where public space becomes participatory, where people appropriate the space and develop a sense of community and identity.

Our designs reflect how spaces relate to each other; the type of identity they create and how they interrelate with the historical and material context. A space has many readings; as a program and as an atmosphere; text and subtext. Design, for us, is a way to materialize an idea, but also to think and experience it; a perceptual game that blurs the border between reality and fiction.

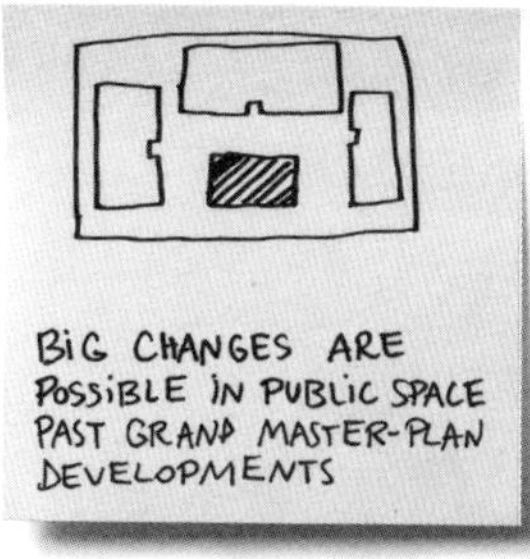

To strategically think about available space and the way it accommodates time is one of the architect´s most significant capacities.

An architect works with a purpose, but allows enough room for change, and always takes the initiative to propose solutions.

Architects, as professionals in their fields, can detect, frame, source and solve problems, which may be blind spots to significant stakeholders and policy-makers.

Place-making, an essential component in an architects practice, is the results of asking what their role regarding community building is.

The architect plays the role of mediator-provocateur-manager between institutions and the community. In many cases, we have noted that design, for both, seems superfluous. However, we maintain that beauty is not a luxury, does not imply a higher cost or is opposed to the functionality of a space, on the contrary, we have confirmed that it improves the quality of life.

For us, design is a creative and strategic thinking process aimed at offering better aesthetic and functional solutions to complex human problems. By taking the initiative of identifying a problem, probing and persuading others to find a feasible solution, we contribute to society as designers. Imagination is coupled to experimentation and method to resolution.

"it is a mark of success in a park, public lobby or a porch, when people can come there and fall asleep.

make these places

keep the environment filled with ample benches, comfortable places, corners to sit on the ground, or lie in comfort in the sand.

relatively sheltered, protected from circulation

perhaps up a step, with seats and grass to slump down upon, read the paper
and
doze

off."

Christopher Alexander

ROUTE

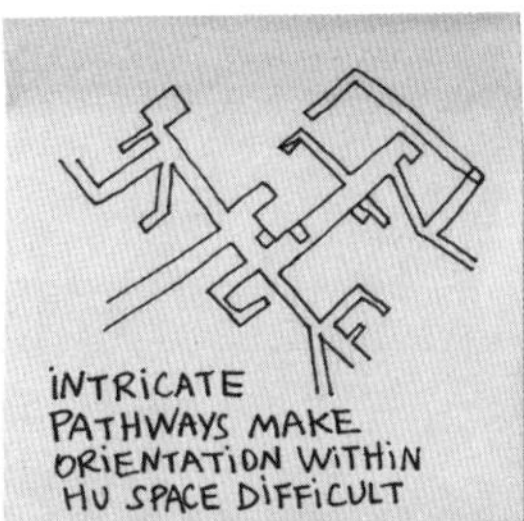

Active junctions, where many paths converge, become exciting intersections for people, more so than usual crosswalks.

In general, people choose the shortest, straightest and straightest, safest and best-lit path.

Underused land is the passage between two colonies, that, on certain weekends, becomes a soccer field. The traces of people mark the path that generates different uses.
All routes generate a spatial reading. The ways of transiting spaces determine their own reading.

Walking through illuminated roads lines decreases violence in parks and public spaces, it improves neighborhood connections, circulation and safety, reactivating community's disposition for recreation.

Fresnillo Playground: Housing Unit public space project by REA, Fresnillo, Zacatecas, 2017

"Architecture also has to do with sound, but not with pragmatic sound but with supernatural sound, the sound of the soul. When you enter a building, it gives you the wavelength of its sound. It is something that characterizes the best architecture of all time."

John Hejduk

SOUND

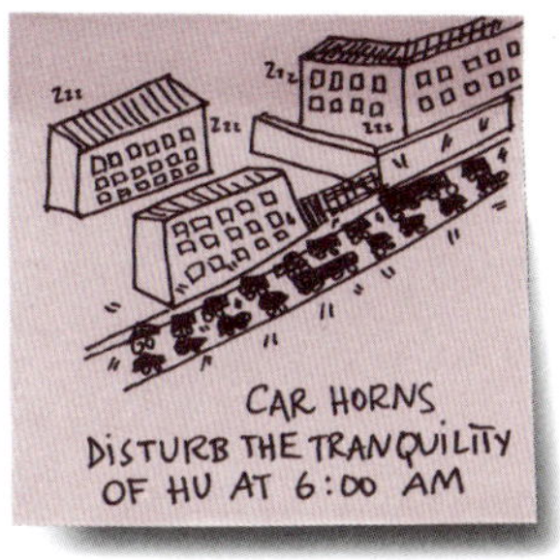

Hawkers' street-cries and chantings are an essential part of the sound heritage of the city, aural space and temporality compasses: city clocks that regulate the life of commercial hubs.

Using aural, spatial illusions, the daily mobility of the HU hawkers show the manifold urban readings and layers comprised in their regular exchanges.

The atmosphere of any space, full of sounds and meanings, creates sensations, experiences, memories, and presences.

transform space into place

"a place where someone can
make a graceful or dramatic
entrance

a place from which to speak

a place from which to look at
other people while also being
seen

a place which increases face to
face contact when many people
are together

a special place to sit ."

Christopher Alexander

VERTICAL

YYYYYYYYYYYYYYY
YYYYYYYYYYYYYYY
YYYYYYYYYYYYYYY
YYYYYYYYYYYYYYY
YYYYYYYYYYYYYYY
YYYYYYYYYYYYYYY
YYYYYYYYYYYYYYY
YYYYYYYYYYYYYYY
YYYYYYYYYYYYYYY
YYYYYYYYYYYYYYY
YYYYYYYYYYYYYYY
YYYYYYYYYYYYYYY
YYYYYYYYYYYYYYY
YYYYYYYYYYYYYYY
YYYYYYYYYYYYYYY
YYYYYYYYYYYYYYY
YYYYYYYYYYYYYYY
YYYYYYYYYYYYYYY
YYYYYYYYYYYYYYY
YYYYYYYYYYYYYYY
YYYYYYYYYYYYYYY
YYYYYYYYYYYYYYY
YYYYYYYYYYYYYYY
YYYYYYYYYYYYYYY
YYYYYYYYYYYYYYY
YYYYYYYYYYYYYYY
YYYYYYYYYYYYYYY

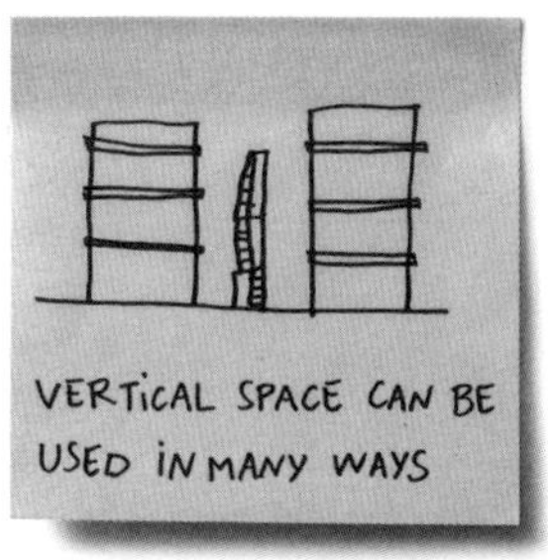

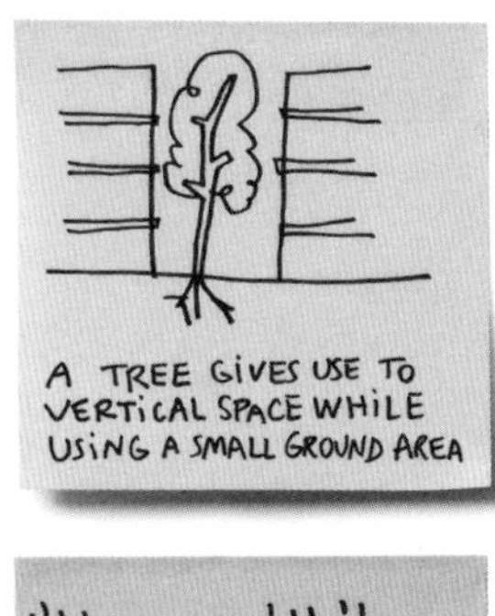

HORIZONTAL

XXXXXXXXXXXXXXXXXXXXXXXXXXXXXXX
XXXXXXXXXXXXXXXXXXXXXXXXXXXXXXX
XXXXXXXXXXXXXXXXXXXXXXXXXXXXXXX
XXXXXXXXXXXXXXXXXXXXXXXXXXXXXXX
XXXXXXXXXXXXXXXXXXXXXXXXXXXXXXX
XXXXXXXXXXXXXXXXXXXXXXXXXXXXXXX

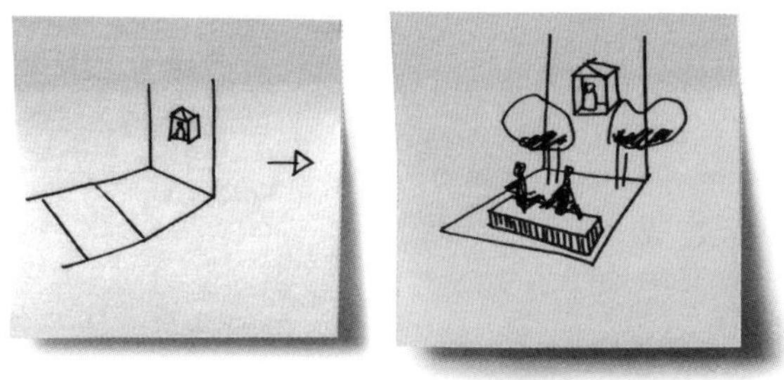

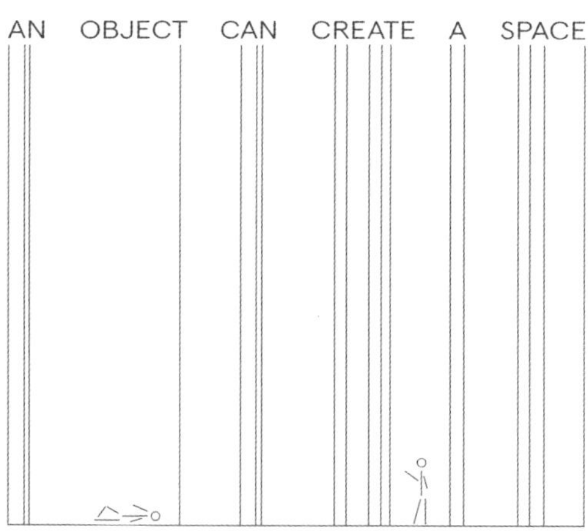
AN OBJECT CAN CREATE A SPACE

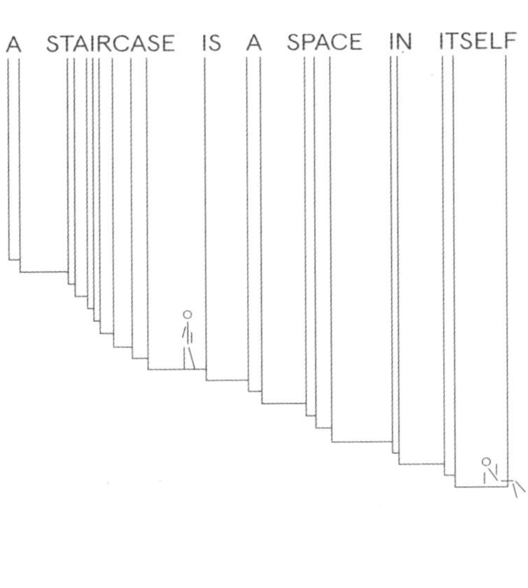
A STAIRCASE IS A SPACE IN ITSELF

F5

Common-Unity: Housing Unit public space project by REA, Azcapotzalco, Mexico City, 2015-2016

In the past twenty years, many social housing projects with no public spaces design whatsoever have been delivered by real estate developers. The results are obsolete, unsustainable housing units, which requires an urgent re-thinking approach.

"Somewhere in every garden, there must be at least one spot, a quiet garden seat, in which a person - or two people - can reach into themselves and be in touch with nothing else but nature."

Christopher Alexander

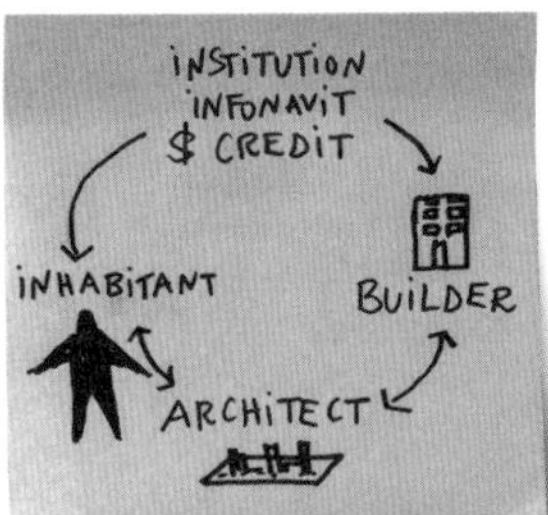

Now, people talk about "social and resilient architecture", in many cases, in a glib and superficial way. However, when the designer works with the community, he encourages co-responsibility, shares design tools so that the social fabric is re-articulated, allowing architecture to act and respond in sustainable, effective and necessary ways.

The "healing effect" of HU is immediate: when public areas become anchors for resilience and equity, hubs for ecological awareness and biodiversity preservation.

Sustainability sustains habilities.

Reactivating of misused or underused public area has demonstrated to us that community engagement is a critical factor for sustainability.

A PROJECT IS NOT
ONLY ITS PLAN DESIGN

WHAT COUNTS
IS HOW YOU LIVE

TEMPORALITY

T

Understanding the factors that expand the functions of a site based on a temporal and multifunctional approach transforms a community space and gives it identity and character.

Temporary transformation of public space acknowledges new social dynamics and uses of a space for instance when a street market is set.

Architectural space configures a vision of time. The use of space may be ephemeral, semi-temporary or permanent.

Mobile and temporal uses of space articulate a different culture in the urban scale.

Our methodology redefines the architectural syntax of space and emphasizes the role that temporality plays in urban design.

6:30 AM

7:00 AM

7:30 AM

9:30 AM

10:00 AM

10:30 AM

12:30 AM

1:00 PM

1:30 PM

3:30 PM

4:00 PM

4:30 PM

6:30 PM

7:00 PM

7:30 PM

9:30 PM

10:00 PM

10:30 PM

8:00 AM

8:30 AM

9:00 AM

11:00 AM

11:30 AM

12:00 AM

2:00 PM

2:30 PM

3:00 PM

5:00 PM

5:30 PM

6:00 PM

8:00 PM

8:30 PM

9:00 PM

11:00 PM

11:30 PM

12:00 PM

Common-Unity: Housing Unit public space project by REA, Azcapotzalco, Mexico City, 2015–2016

T E X T

T E X T

T E X T

T E X T

CONTEXT

CONTEXT

CONTEXT

CONTEXT

CONTEXT

CONTEXT

CONTEXT

T E X T
E   E
X   X
T E X T

C C C C C C C C C C C C C C
O O O O O O O O O O O O O O
N N N N N N N N N N N N N N
T T T T T T T T T T T T T T
E E E E E E E E E E E E E E
X X X X X X X X X X X X X X
T T T T T T T T T T T T T T

TOPOGRAPHY

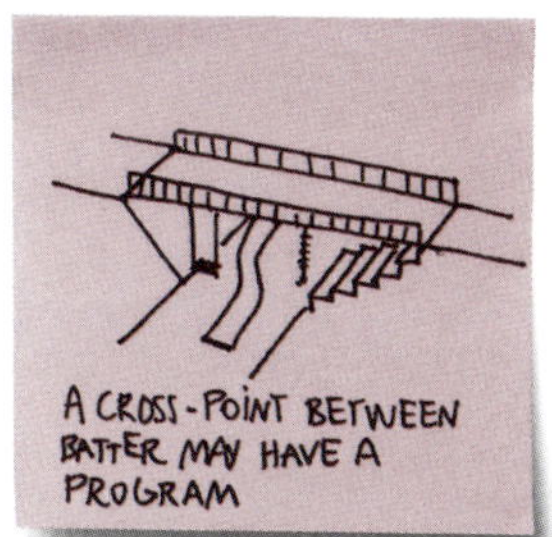

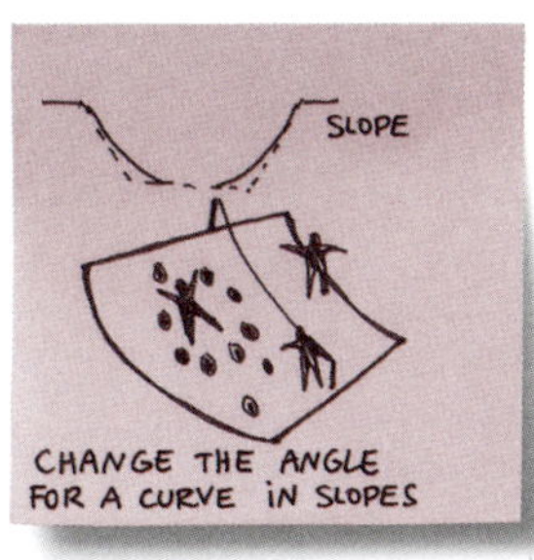

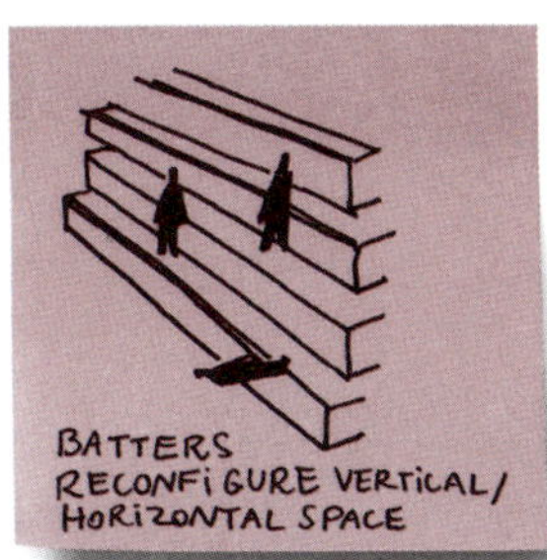

When a derelict, underused or disused urban space is addressed as simple topography, unclaimed characteristics of the territory can be re-signified and turned into areas that give a new dimension to social tensions of a given environment.
In the process of making a city, topographic maps are represented with their different variables: surfaces, reliefs, elevations, depths, distances and directions that acquire three-dimensional value when superimposed on each other.
Design that curates a sense of place; reshapes the cultural landscape: it helps people redefine their notion of territory through togetherness rather than transience.
Our strategy has always been to recycle and re-signify the existing infrastructure of a site. Rather than generate a landscape to a program, we transform the existing urban landscape into the program.

CROSS-POINT

WALKS

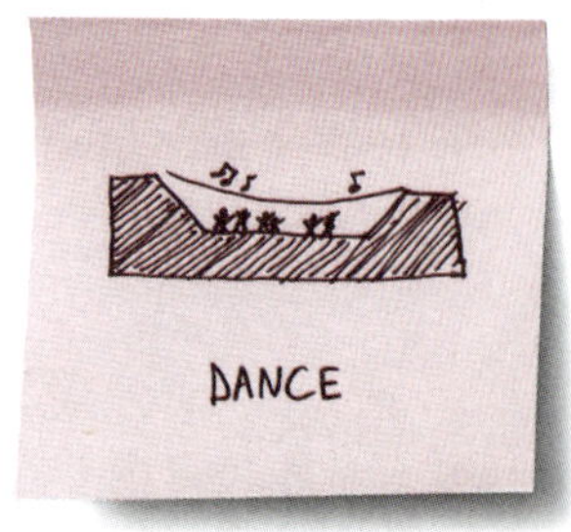
DANCE

CLOTHES-LINES
CONCERTS
MARKETS

Fresnillo Playground: Housing Unit public space project by REA, Fresnillo, Zacatecas, 2017

OPEN SPACES ARE
SPACES IN AND OF
THEMSELVES

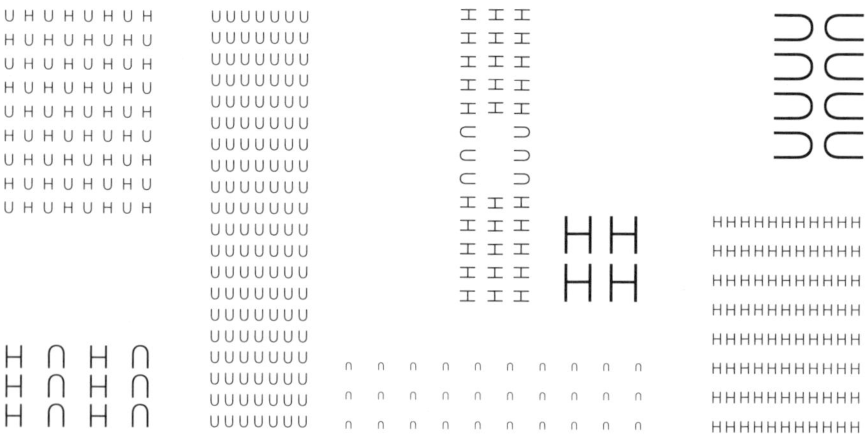

TYPOLOGY

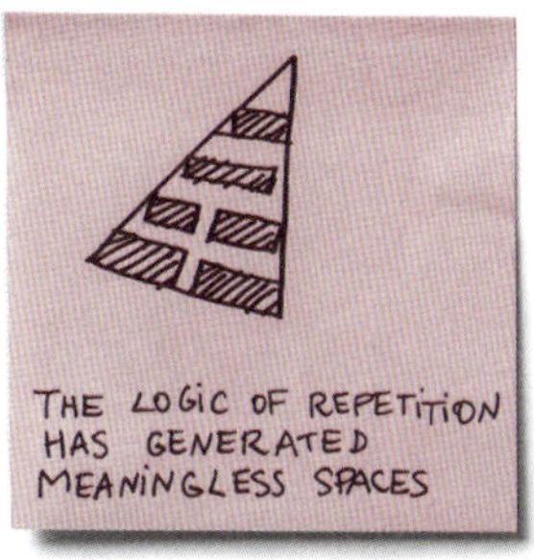
THE LOGIC OF REPETITION
HAS GENERATED
MEANINGLESS SPACES

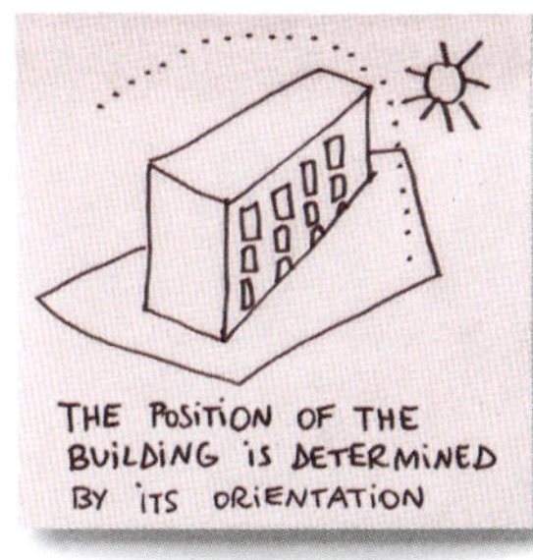
THE POSITION OF THE
BUILDING IS DETERMINED
BY ITS ORIENTATION

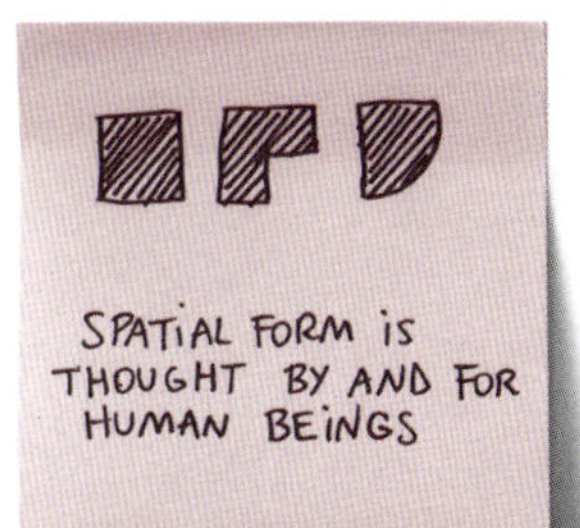
SPATIAL FORM IS
THOUGHT BY AND FOR
HUMAN BEINGS

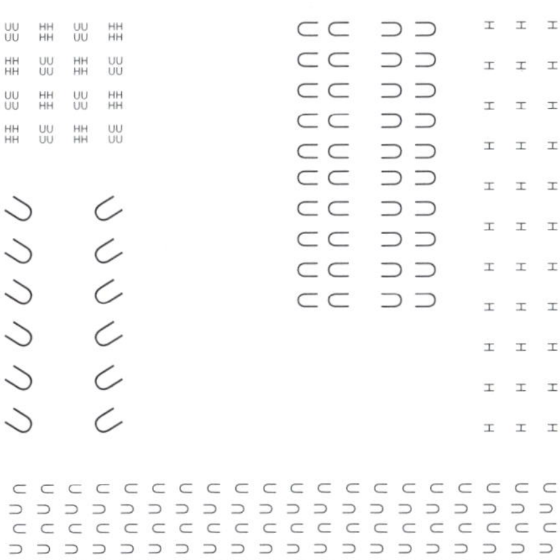

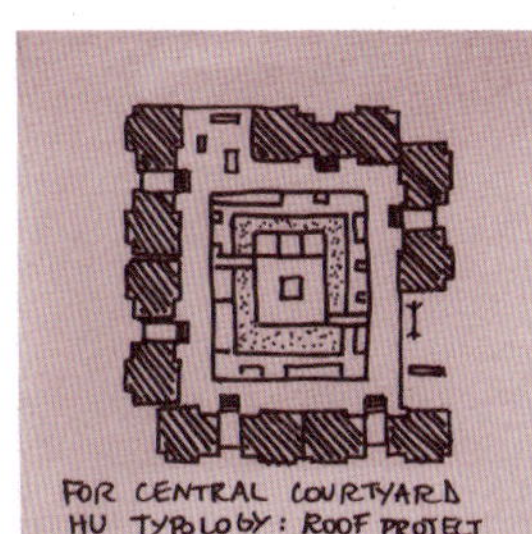
FOR CENTRAL COURTYARD
HU TYPOLOGY: ROOF PROJECT

the backyard
the garden
the little forest
the parking-lot
the pathway
the walking esplanade
the median
the step
the stairs
the street lighting
the lamp
the goalkeeper
the pavement
the pergola
the tree
the bush
the grass
the light
the shadow
the puddle
the cement
the soil
the car
the shrine
the bike
the fence
the dog
the cat
the cabin
the wall
the neighbor
the lock
the flowerpots
the plants
the doors
the light-bulbs
the party
the playground
the promenade
the barbecue
the meeting
the gaze
the concert
the ceremony
the pause
the exploration
the thingamajig
the people cleaning
the repair-job
the work-out
the walk
the reading
the water-jug
the nap
the meeting
the sun-day
the rain
the ropes
the announcements

USES

WINDOWS ARE DECORATED

ROOFTOPS CAN HAVE DIFFERENT USES

HU RESIDENTS USE AND INHABIT NEARBY PUBLIC AREAS

PLACING FURNITURE DOES NOT IMPLY ACTIVITY

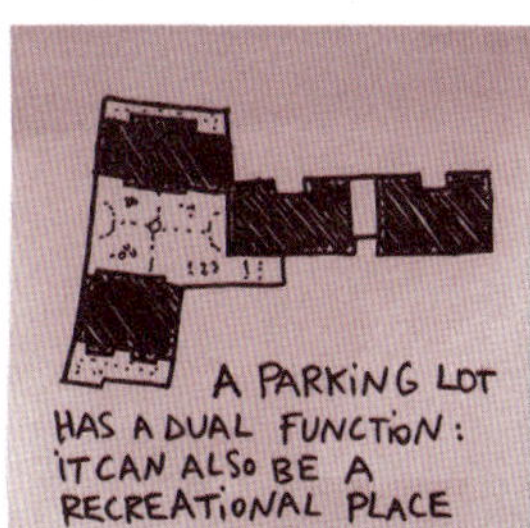
A PARKING LOT HAS A DUAL FUNCTION: IT CAN ALSO BE A RECREATIONAL PLACE

COMMON SPACE HAPPENINGS DO NOT HAPPEN ELSEWHERE

Court: Housing Unit public space project by REA, Lagos de Puente Moreno, Veracruz, 2016

When areas of vegetation require regular maintenance, they end up as vacant lots, full of garbage, abandoned and became propitious for illicit activities.

It is a common mistake to replace green spaces with concrete plates to reduce maintenance costs; depriving inhabitants the chance to experience the changing seasons to sit in the shade of a tree.

Rainwater absorption and avoiding floods are essential characteristics of the green spaces in any HU public space.

VEGETATION

V

The agora-portico creates with vegetation a new habitat and expands the user's program by way of height and inter-column-capacity.

Common areas become a hub for ecological awareness and biodiversity preservation.

Landscape and nature are also real constituents of space.

The vegetation can fill, invade, beautify or desert a space.

The roots, invisible space/volume of plants, must always be considered. Without a significant amount of earth a tree won't grow properly. The proximity of a reduced soil for a green space to paved area, produce unevenness, cracks, and rupture of installations; therefore, the inhabitants of HU's, in general, prefer to eliminate vegetation and green spaces.

Vegetation enriches the open space in the HU with multiple possibilities: patio with a tree, pergolas, small garden, miniature forest, climbing plants in walls.

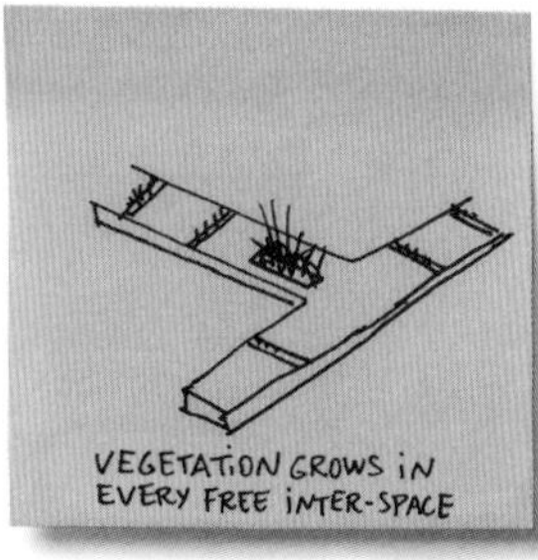

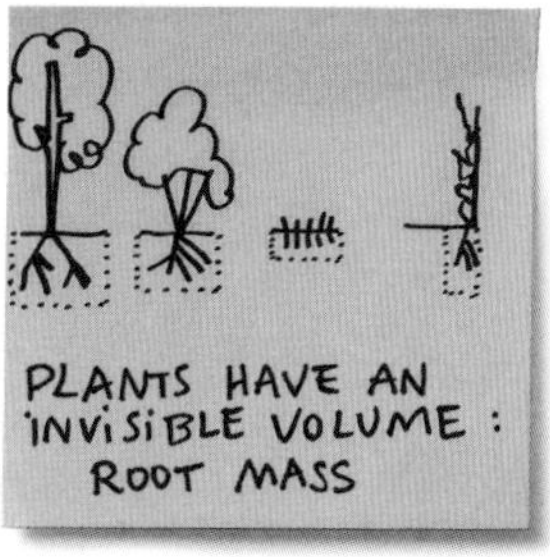

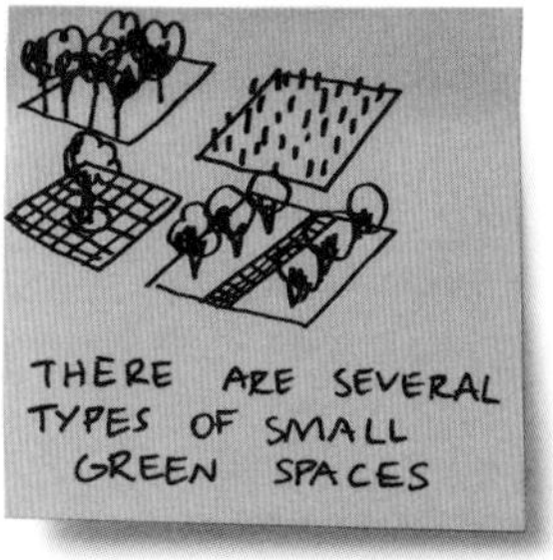

Common-Unity: Housing Unit public space project by REA, Azcapotzalco, Mexico City, 2015-2016

VOID

V

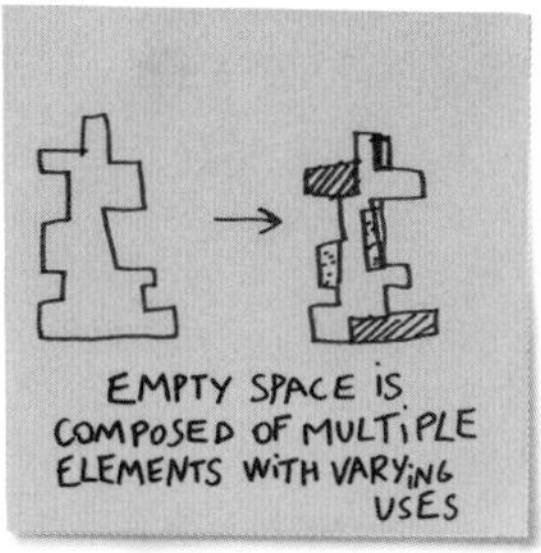
EMPTY SPACE IS
COMPOSED OF MULTIPLE
ELEMENTS WITH VARYING
USES

1
2
3
COMMON AREAS ARE THE
RESULT OF RESIDUAL SPACES
RATHER THAN PLANNED
STRUCTURAL COMPONENTS

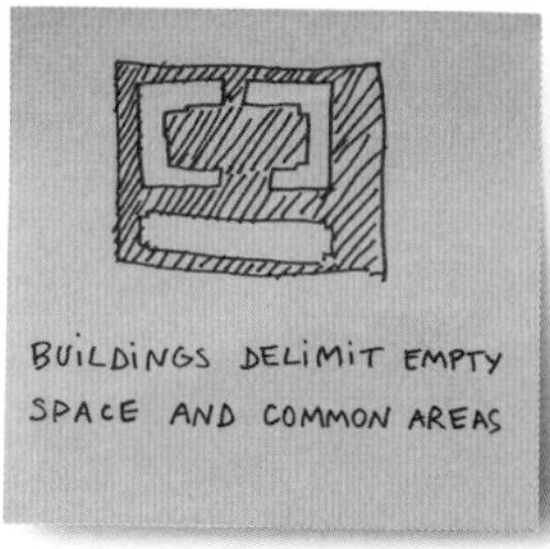
BUILDINGS DELIMIT EMPTY
SPACE AND COMMON AREAS

WATER CAN SUGGEST
A PLAYGROUND

DOOR-ACCESS ROOFS
SHELTER FROM THE RAIN

In the rehabilitation of the HU it is necessary to establish a logic for water conduction: guide its ways to infiltration areas with the help of a topographic study.

Mexico City has a serious water supply problem, and it lacks a saving and recollecting culture.

Designing water collectors can become a pedagogical tool; built and operated by the community they could spark the necessity of the water shortage awareness.

In a city where every time it rains, the sewage system become saturated, it is important to look for alternatives to guide the water. In open spaces the solution is, in general, to recover and infiltrate rainwater.

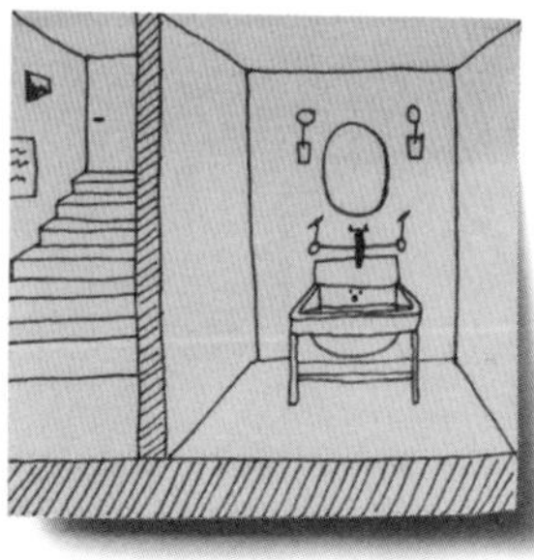

X RAYS

To radiograph a building, layers must be removed.

The facade is equivalent to the skin; the materials to the muscles; the installations to the organs; and the structure to the bones.

The procedure of extraction of layers allows a diagnosis of the state of health of dwellings, as well as the habits, routines and customs of the people, to understand the needs of design in depth.

We see buildings as knowledge structures. And as such, they become models of new knowledge, collective memory and understating.

We explore how architecture materializes in meaningful structures to reflect new meanings and syntaxes.

Housing Units after the 7/S and 19/S deadly earthquakes, Jojutla, Mexico, 2017

Y

Y

Never underestimate the power of the line to redefine space.

Drawing a single line can create a new public space; it is an ephemeral and determining tool in architectural design.

A line can transform a barren ground into a playground.

A single line may help rebuild people´s perception of space, its uses and traditions as well as the memory of a community.

More than following a line of design, our challenge has been to make the line a presence, a vector, a force. By activating its strength, it organizes, mobilizes and generates change.

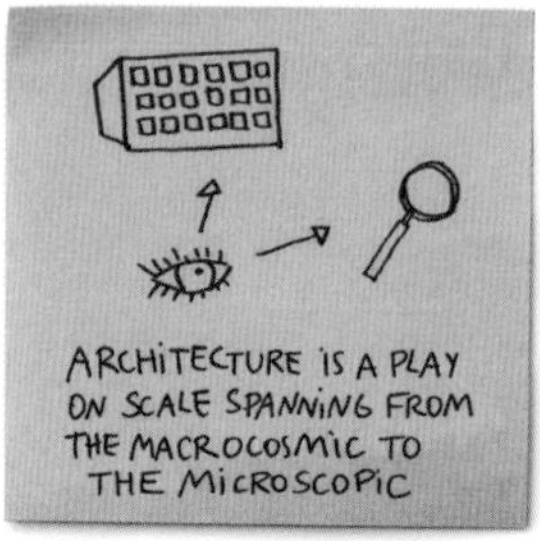
ARCHITECTURE IS A PLAY ON SCALE SPANNING FROM THE MACROCOSMIC TO THE MICROSCOPIC

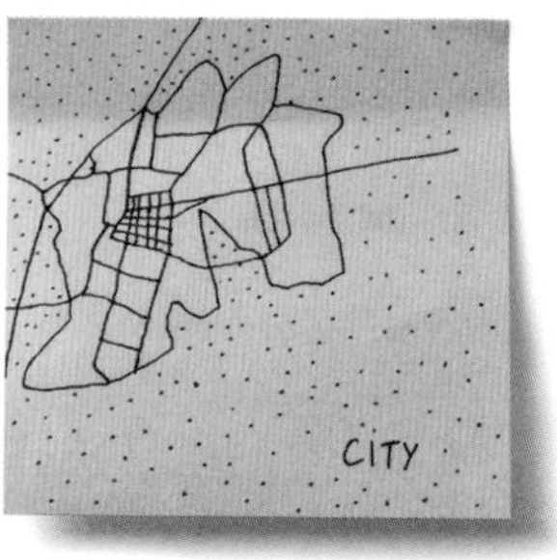
CITY

NEIGHBORHOOD

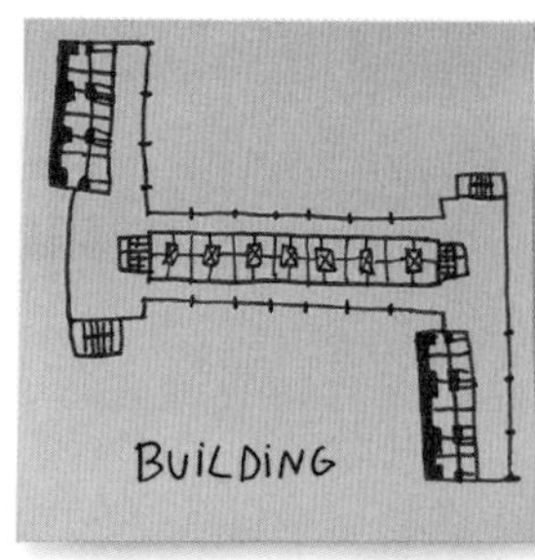
BUILDING

ZOOM

Zoom enables multiple readings due to scale superposition.

A visual-spatial metaphor occurs where the macro-scale becomes possible in a microcosm.

Our research proves that the ecotone implies negotiations between the public and private sphere, it mitigates the change from open to enclosed areas and allows a peaceful coexistence between natural and urbanized areas. Likewise, it links different scales and layers of space (from local to regional), promotes social diversity, manages mobility, regulates times in the use of space, connects and facilitates an efficient use of resources. The public space and the architecture we design enables space to become aware, both for change and exchange.

F1

Common-Unity: Housing Unit public space project by REA, Azcapotzalco, Mexico City, 2015-2016

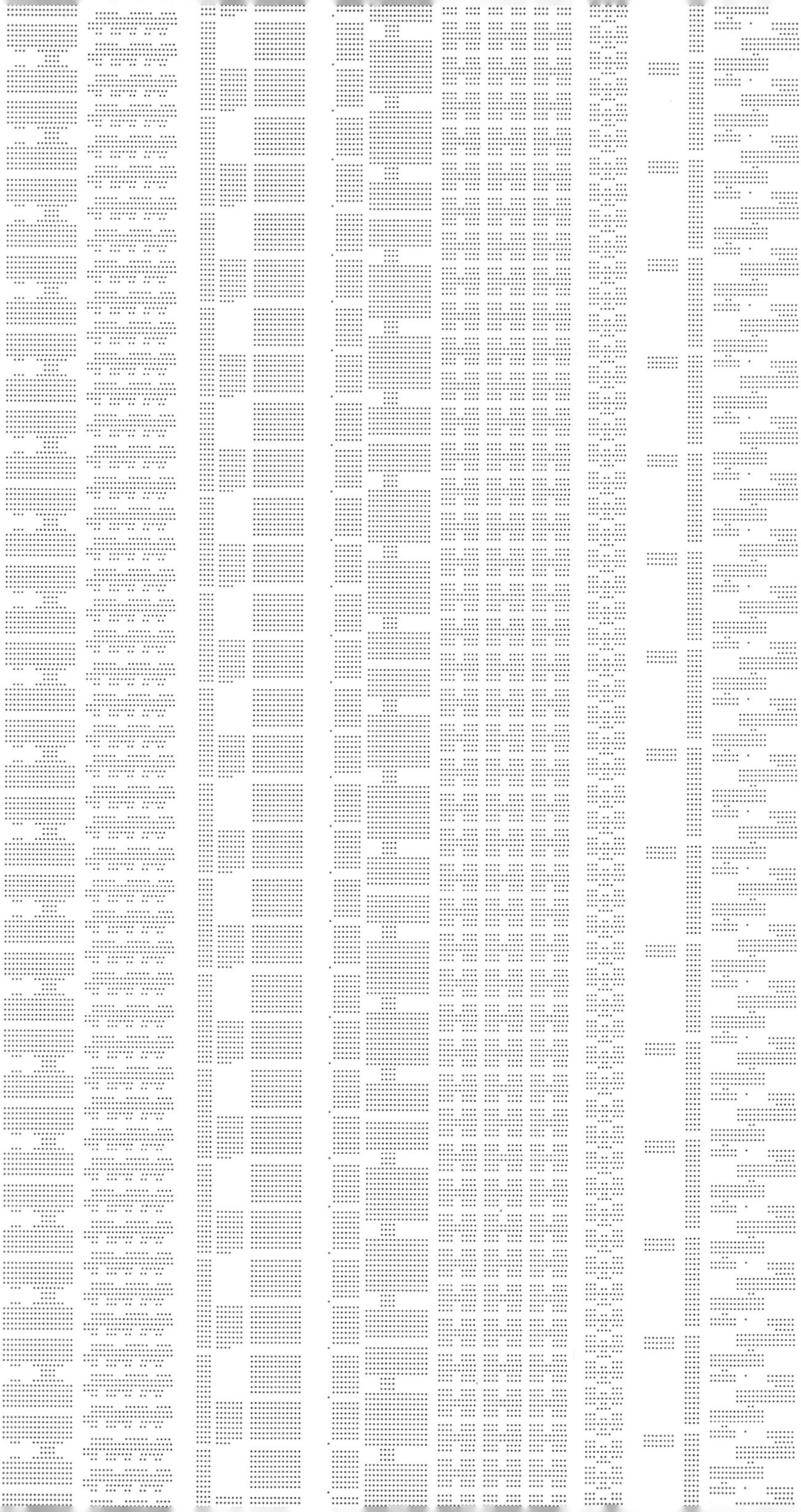

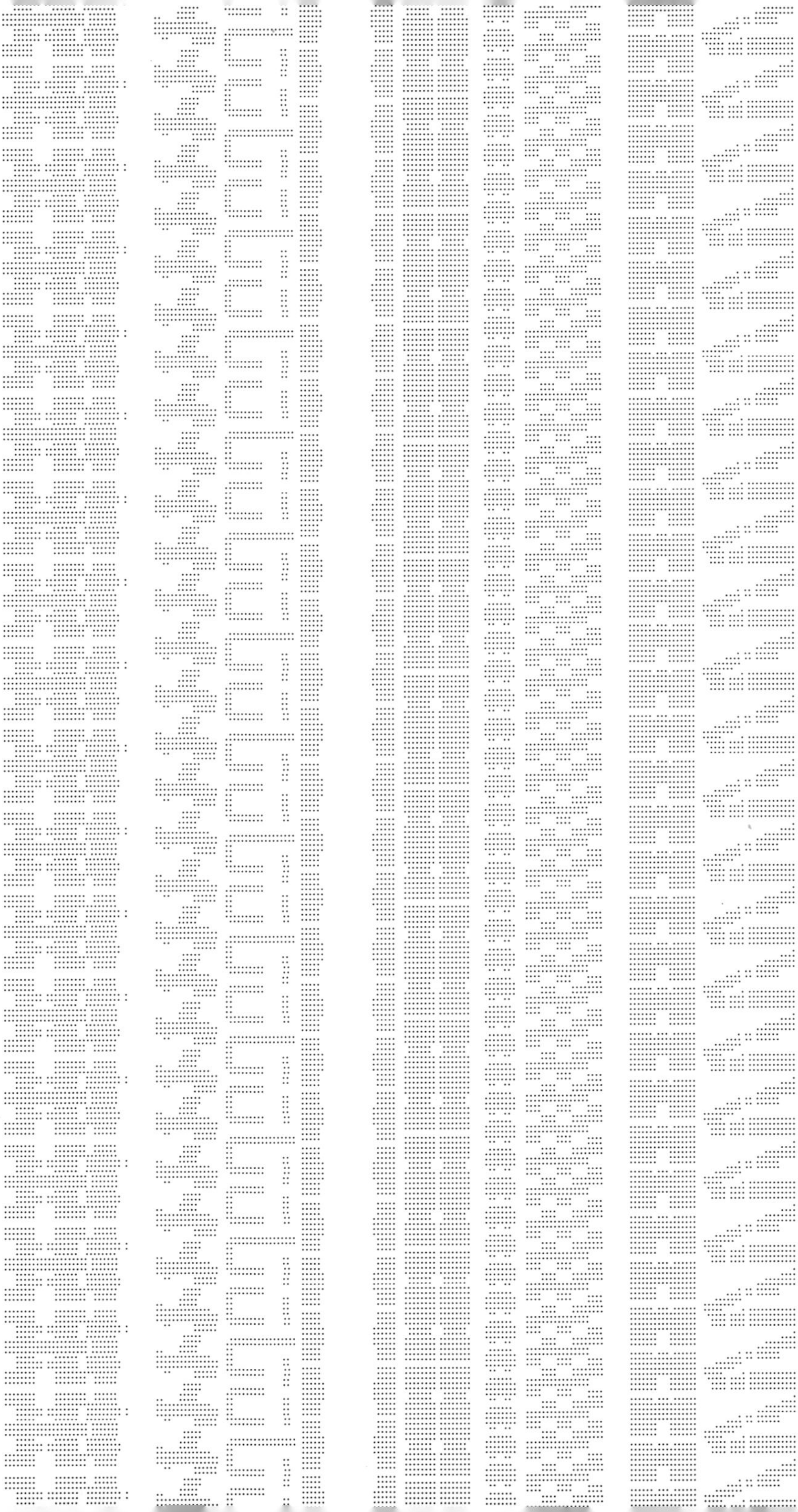

Mexico City's Housing Units Footprints

MANIFESTO

3 PROJECTS

COMMON-UNITY + EL SALONCITO

COURT

FRESNILLO PLAYGROUND

MANIFESTO

We free the potential of space to become a place. To achieve place-making:

1. We seek content in context

Before setting out to design, we thoroughly research the specific potential, resources, community assets and essential needs of a site. Our architectural solutions create new situations that transform a site into a place. Our design strategies engage people, not as consumers of space, but as place-makers.

2. We change barriers into boundaries

One of our design strategies to reclaim privatized spaces for public use has been to replace vertical elements (railing, walls, gates, enclosures) which separate and divide, with horizontal elements (roof, floors, shelter, passageway) that connect, reunite, open access, bring closer together and encourage social interaction. The margins between inner space and outer space, private space and public space can be flexibly managed by the users.

3. We shift spatial perception

Through site-actions, we draw on the assets and skills of a community, and combine them with professional expertise to attain innovative results. We define site-action as a public space intervention designed to involve users in ways that creatively free space from preconceptions.

4. We approach the landscape as the program

Derelict, underused or disused urban space are approached as natural topographies. Unclaimed urban spaces can be transformed into places of resilience, inclusive and rich in function diversity. By recycling and re-signifying extant infrastructure we transform an urban scar or hostile border of the landscape into an attractive horizon.

5. We re-signify materials

Textures and atmospheres are essential in creating a sense of place. Our re-reading of color, natural local materials, or industrial materials through patterns, surfaces and shapes, is sensitive to users' experience of habitability. The materiality of our design is an invitation to look closer.

6. We work with temporality

Our public space design considers the aging of building materials; the transformations of user needs over time that involve resilient re-appropriations of space; the use of space through-out the day by different segments of the population; the wealth of making space for the serendipity.

7. We hold beauty as a basic right

Beautiful design is an investment in dignity. Regardless of budgetary constraints, good designers make beauty affordable by a virtuous allocation of resources. Elegant solutions are intrinsic to the program. Aesthetic decisions can change people's lives. Approach every space with the same respect you have for revered places.

before

after

COMMON-UNITY

MEXICO CITY

COMMON-UNITY is a public space rehabilitation project in the San Pablo Xalpa housing unit, Mexico City. By taking a place-making approach, we transformed the alienated sectors of the housing complex into a community of BARRIOS—what we termed COMMON-UNITY. We worked around the physical barriers created by the residents in common areas to make them permeable, democratic and meaningful. Through participatory planning, our design strategy substituted dividing vertical structures for sheltering horizontal ones: we implemented roof-modules equipped for a diverse program (blackboards, climbing walls, handrails and nets). The new design spoke for itself: residents agreed to remove 90% of the barriers and the recovered public space became an extension of each apartment. The new space facilitated a different kind of ownership and appropriation: one that habituates inhabitants to work for the common good.

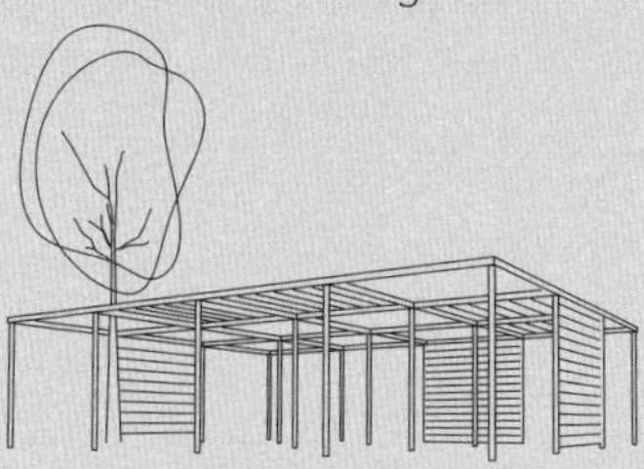

Location: San Pablo Xalpa Housing Unit, Azcapotzalco, Mexico City
Program: Public Space and Library
Built: 2015-2016
Collaboration: Alin Wallach
Client: Infonavit, SHF, CONAVI

before

after

SALONCITO

MEXICO CITY

We found an old leaky warehouse that had already become a multipurpose room for school tutoring, knitting clubs and religious instruction. The people wanted to enlarge the room to expand their activity program. So we redesigned it all together to make it a functional warm space taking into account their program of activities. A bookstore donated an important collection of children books and this became a library. We went from a leaky ware-house to a sunny library reading room. We focused on developing integral low-cost improvement of these place and gave back to the people a sense of community and gathering together.

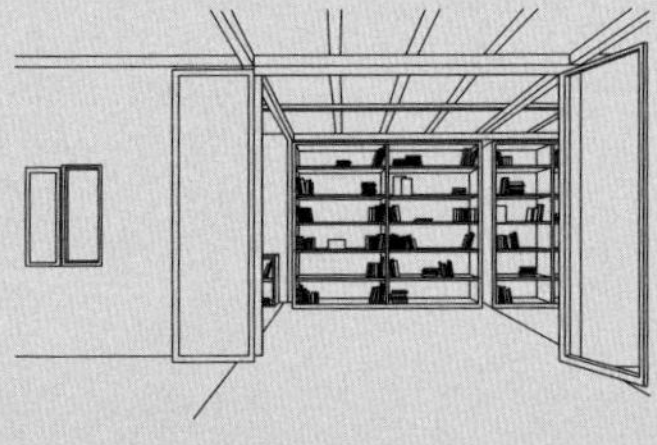

Location: San Pablo Xalpa Housing Unit, Azcapotzalco, Mexico City
Program: Public Space and Library
Built: 2015-2016
Collaboration: Alin Wallach
Client: Infonavit, SHF, CONAVI

before

after

COURT

VERACRUZ, MEXICO

For a suburban residential complex near the port of Veracruz, we designed a sports court that houses an entire community center. The portico is more than a roof: it uses the inter-column capacity of the construction to generate a varied activity program (shops, multifunctional rooms, balconies, terraced seating, kids recreational areas, hammock area, adult fitness room, activity rooms, bathroom). The use of latticework and palm wood reproduce the seaside atmosphere of the nearby a coast. In the agora, designed to complement the portico, we introduced local trees and vegetation to shade and cool the area (comprised by forum, skateboard park and picnic area). The new habitat has become a hub for ecological awareness and biodiversity preservation.

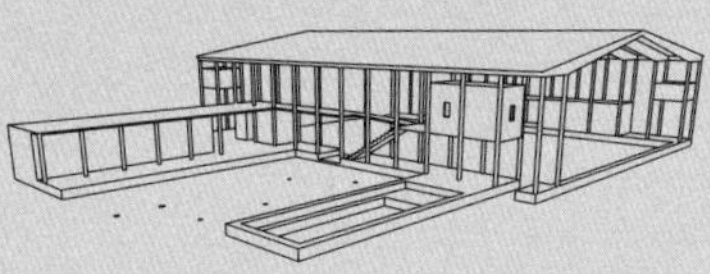

Location: Lagos de Puente Moreno, Veracruz
Program: Court and Plaza
Built: 2016
Collaboration: Alin Wallach
Client: Infonavit

before

after

FRESNILLO PLAYGROUND

ZACATECAS, MEXICO

We recycled a paved sewage canal and transformed it into a playground for a housing unit in Fresnillo, Zacatecas. The new transitional space offers a safe recreational area and welcomes the public to a new habitat of local vegetation. The bridge, floor and slopes we designed are equipped for a multi-functional program. We made universally accessible bridges that opened an esplanade underneath; and rebuilt the canal slopes to make them work as a resting area, agora steps and a playground program of climbing walls. The new space improves the life quality of the overall housing complex and offers opportunity to groups in situations of risk. Recycling the extant infrastructure transformed an urban scar into an attractive horizon: the cityscape became the program.

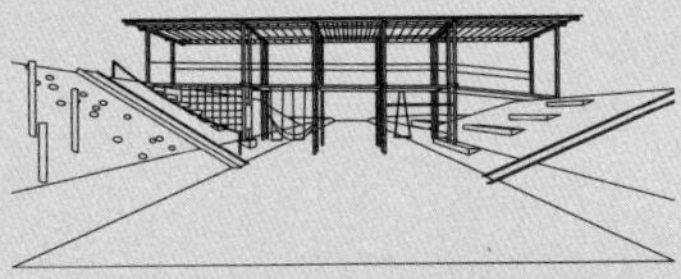

Location: Manuel M. Ponce Housing Unit, Zacatecas, Mexico.
Program: Public Space and Playground
Built: 2017
Collaboration: Alin Wallach
Client: Infonavit

P L A C E

S P A C E

B L A N K

S P A C E

E M P T Y

S P A C E

Rozana Montiel is the founder of the firm ROZANA MONTIEL | ESTUDIO DE ARQUITECTURA specialized in architectural design, artistic re-conceptualizations of space, and the public domain. The studio works with a wide variety of projects on different scales and layers that range from the city to the micro-object, artifacts and books.

Special thanks to:

The Rockefeller Foundation
Bellagio Center

Mauricio Gómez de Tuddo
Jana Gómez Montiel
Carlos Zedillo Velasco
Miquel Adrià
Verónica Martínez Lira
Hortense Blanchard
Enrique Giner de los Ríos
Sandra Pereznieto
Jaime Navarro
Erika Manning Márquez
Claudia Rodríguez
Josefa Díaz Cardoso
Ombeline de Laage
Francisca López Pani
Giulia Anserini
Karina Caballero
Adriana Rodríguez
Camille Rouzaud

And to everyone who helped make this book possible.

This work was printed thanks to the support of the Instituto del Fondo Nacional de la Vivienda para los Trabajadores, Infonavit.

This book was published as part of "La Biennale Architettura di Venezia 2018".

HU
Common Spaces in Housing Units
First edition in English, 2018
Second reprint, 2021

www.rozanamontiel.com

Barranca del Muerto 280,
Colonia Guadalupe Inn,
Delegación Álvaro Obregón,
Ciudad de Mexico, 01029
ISBN 978-607-96505-9-9

Rozana Montiel
estudio de arquitectura

Author
Rozana Montiel

Graphic Concept, Design and Post its
Rozana Montiel
Louise Rouzaud

Contribution
Hortense Blanchard

Texts
Rozana Montiel
Yaoci Pardo

Copy Editor
Verónica Martínez Lira

Translations
María Teresa Gerard
Yaoci Pardo

Photography
Sandra Pereznieto:
pages 24, 35, 50, 54, 59, 64, 69, 73, 86, 95, 100, 101, 104, 127, 138, 153, 156, 170, 176, 177, 184, 190, 195, 210, 218, 220, 222
Jaime Navarro:
pages 76, 109, 146, 162, 176, 177, 224
Rozana Montiel estudio de arquitectura:
pages 4, 5, 21, 28, 34, 42, 43, 46, 79, 90, 122, 131, 140, 176, 177, 204, 218, 220, 222, 224

Post-its photography
Erika Manning Márquez

Infonavit

General Director
David Penchyna Grub

Head of the Research Center of Sustainable Development
Carlos Zedillo Velasco

Arquine, S.A. de C.V.
Ámsterdam 163 A
Colonia Hipódromo,
Delegación Cuauhtémoc,
Ciudad de México, 06100
www.arquine.com

Arquine

Director
Miquel Adrià

Chief Editor
Selene Patlán

Publication Coordinator
Brisna Zaragoza

Layout Adjustments
Samuel Morales

Proofreading
Quentin Pope

Prepress
Emilio Breton

ROZANA MONTIEL
ESTUDIO DE
ARQUITECTURA

INFONAVIT

Arquine

This book was printed and bound in August 2021 by Offset Santiago in Mexico. It was set in typefaces of the Avenir Next Pro and Apercu families. The print run was 500 copies.